Moving
To Courage

Transcendent Moments of Change
in the Lives of Women

CHERYL FISCHER
&
HEATHER WAITE

WILDCAT CANYON PRESS
A Division of Circulus Publishing Group, Inc.
Berkeley, California

Moving From Fear to Courage: Transcendent Moments of Change in the Lives of Women

Publisher: Tamara Traeder
Editorial Director: Roy M. Carlisle
Marketing Director: Carol Brown
Managing Editor: Leyza Yardley
Production Coordinator: Larissa Berry
Copyeditor: Jean Blomquist
Proofreader: Shirley Coe
Cover Photographs: SPL/Photonica
Cover Design: Mary Beth Salmon
Interior Design & Typesetting: Terragraphics/Margaret Copeland
Typographic Specifications: Body type set in StempelSchneidler 11/16 and Triplex Serif Light 11/16. Heads set in StempelSchneidler Medium and Triplex Serif Bold.

Printed in Canada

Library of Congress Cataloging-in-Publication Data
Fischer, Cheryl, 1952-
    Moving from fear to courage : transcendent movements of change
  in the lives of women / Cheryl Fischer & Heather Waite
        p. cm.
    ISBN 1-885171-50-1 (alk. paper)
      1. Women—Psychology. 2. Life change events. 3. Fear. I. Waite,
Heather, 1957- II. Title.

HQ1206.F48 2001
179'.6'082—dc21   2001017894

Distributed to the trade by Publishers Group West
10 9 8 7 6 5 4 3 2 1

Contents

Dedication

In memory of Dr. Benjamin Levine

Acknowledgments

We are grateful to all of the women who so graciously came forth and courageously shared their stories with us. Without you and your willingness to be heard, this book would never have been possible. We also deeply thank Kathy Lahijani, Barbara Morris, Karen Delaney, Sheryl Bard, Chris M. Wood, Sherry McCoy, Arline Halper, Anna Maria Thomasillo, Peg Seegers, Kimberly Carvalho, Ana Chacon, Anny Rusk, Gina Agee, Deborah Hak, Debbie Lockie, and Penny Jacobs for their generous fearlessness and for being our soul sisters divine.

Cheryl: I would like to thank my coauthor, Heather Waite, for her effervescent spirit and creative spark. I also thank my parents, Jean and Cy Smythe, who taught me love and the tenacity to hold onto it. I give a big hug to my colleagues at Ryokan College, as well as my family and friends who have encouraged this project with their curiosity and excitement. I also owe a debt of gratitude to our editor, Roy M. Carlisle, who allowed us to find our own way with this book, and never lost faith. And finally, a special thank-you to my husband, Robert M. Fischer—the love of my life—without whose boundless optimism and unconditional support, this book would not have been written.

Heather: I would like to thank my coauthor, Cheryl Fischer, for this mystical and meaningful journey, as well as everyone who provided support during this stressful time. I give a standing ovation to my parents, Oakley and Nita Waite, who provided me with life, and to my saviors of the night—Roy M. Carlisle and Dr. Arnold Horowitz. And lastly to Jerry and Susan Machado who always make everything right.

Thank you to Jean Blomquist and Shirley Coe for their sensitive copyediting work. And special thanks to everyone at Wildcat Canyon Press, especially Carol Brown, Patsy Barich, and Leyza Yardley. Also, thank you to Tamara Traeder who shared an inspiring vision of courage in the early stages of this book's development.

Preface

We didn't know each other very well. We'd met at graduate school and liked each other, but we'd just never spent much time together. When one of our favorite professors became gravely ill, we came together to support each other through the difficult time. We began to share how afraid we were—of losing our teacher and of the many vulnerabilities of life. What is the true meaning of life? How do we keep ourselves going when everything is falling down around us? What can we do to overcome our fears? The more questions we asked, the more we began to reflect upon our own lives and the events that had transpired to bring us together that day . . .

A Word from Cheryl

It was New Year's Eve of 1993 when my beloved cat died, and I was overcome with grief. Within the next month, a long-term romance ended, I lost my job, and I was forced to move to a different area. Hope seemed lost to me. I felt like my life was a perpetual tunnel, and I couldn't find my way to the light. Sometimes I would just get in bed and lie there, not moving, praying for the end. When a friend asked me if I wanted to go skydiving, I readily accepted, even though I am terrified of flying!

Deep in my heart, I believed that that plane ride would be my last.

As I rode up in the tiny, single-engine plane, I remember thinking, "Well, God, whatever happens is up to you." And with that, I jumped into the sky.

However, once I'd jumped, every single cell in my body seemed to be crying out in terror! My eyes were stretched wide with the oncoming gush of air and horror, and I could hardly breathe for the scream that tried to push out of my lips. How could I have done this? How could I have actually chosen death?! As I plunged faster and faster toward the jagged rocks and blood red sands of the Mojave Desert, I knew, more than anything I had ever known, that I wanted to live.

When my parachute opened and I finally landed safely on the ground, I was never again the same. Something within me had been awakened, maybe for the first time. I was so open and receptive to life, I was a new person. The world looked grand and full of possibilities. And it was.

Two weeks later, I met the man of my dreams. Six months later, we were married on a beach in Hawaii. And we have been happily married ever since.

If I hadn't transcended my fear of flying and jumped out of that plane, I never would have realized just how much I wanted to live. Because I realized that, I was able to recognize my future husband. I was able to recognize that I *had* a future.

A Word from Heather

The day we buried my sister, we became a family shattered. When her casket was closed I, too, stopped living, for I dealt with the pain of my sister's death by running as far away from it as I could. The only good thing that occurred as a result of my sister's death was that, twenty years later, the memory of her burial kept me alive.

It was January of 1994. After a day of snow skiing, the van I was riding in fishtailed and rolled. I was ejected from the van and trapped beneath it. I felt the glass and the cold, wet road slicing through my clothes into my back and legs, until we came to a grinding halt. In that instant, I knew a peace unlike any I had ever known. Teetering precariously between life and death, I knew that if I went to sleep, I would never wake up.

What I did not know was that my head was split open, my left hand was nearly cut off, most of my ribs were broken, my clavicle and femur were broken, my lungs were punctured, and I was bleeding to death from seventy-seven different wounds. But worst of all, my spine was injured. As the blood poured out of my body, my peripheral vision was closing in. I thought the sun was going down—but I was dying.

In what could have been the final bridge between two worlds, the image of my parents shoveling dirt in over my grave appeared in my mind. "No! I will not allow them to bury another child!" Breathing out the heavenly numbness, I fought and clawed my way back to consciousness with an indomitable will to live.

The fear of leaving my parents behind to bury a second child was so great that I willed myself to consciousness. Miraculously, I also survived catastrophic injuries. I am grateful to be alive and to *have* a future.

◆　　◆　　◆

For a long moment, we looked at each other, as the effects of what we had both endured resonated deep within us. We realized that what we had in common gave us a rare and remarkable connection. We understood that we'd both found a new and close friend. But we also began to consider something else. If the two of us had experienced a single, transcendent moment when overcoming fear, a moment that had ultimately changed our lives for the better, perhaps other women had as well.

We knew we couldn't be the only two women who had found the courage to change the future by transcending our fears. We suspected that we had discovered something not only profoundly comforting for ourselves, but for others too.

This book is the result of talking with many women who have transcended insurmountable fears by moving from fear to courage. We hope their stories will inspire you and help you to recognize your own unique courage in the midst of your fears.

Courage and Love

*What Scares Women Most
about Relationships?*

Love is a blessing. To feel love, for all its folly and fearsome curves, is to also feel closest to our idea of heaven, even God.

WHAT KIND OF FEAR does love evoke in women? What does love *feel* like? Does it feel like fear? While some women have described love as a wonderful, giddy, head-over-heels sensation, others have felt crushed and broken by love. In fact, love can involve one of our most profound fears: the knife-like pain of a lover's rejection. Even the thought of rejection can scrape our hearts raw and leave our emotions bare and bloodied. At times, love can even make us feel like dying, and some say we would do well to fear love. But is that true?

What happens when we fear love? Long ago love was, if not feared, certainly treated with caution, and marriage was sometimes perceived as a means to an end. In an article for *about.com*, consultants Sheri and Bob Stritof wrote of the history of marriage: "Traditional cultures arranged marriages for couples. The people involved didn't have much to say about the decision. Most couples didn't marry because they were in love. Some marriages were by proxy, some involved a dowry (bride's family giving money or presents to the groom or his family), some required a bride price (the groom or his family giving money or a present to the bride's family), [and] few had any courtship or dating."[1] It seems marriage could be a very serious business, with little room for such an unpredictable, even dangerous force as love.

How do we perceive love now? Do we remain cautious in our relationships? Yes, at times—but for different reasons. Through the years we have gained the freedom to seek a mate for love, not financial consideration. Because we're no longer constrained by the prospect of an arranged marriage, we can make our own decisions when it comes to whom our mate will be.

But how do we choose?

When we make a decision concerning love do we give in to our emotions, our wildest passions? Or do we analyze our future partner's every move? Are we too demanding? Do we have unrealistic expectations? Do we yearn for someone to take care of us? These are some of the questions we face as women. They can be frightening, but we face them because love is at stake. Love, that most wondrous of human traits and aspirations. Love.

The following women have transcended some of their deepest fears regarding love. They have lost it, fought for it, protected it, and walked out on it, but in each case, they found the courage to overcome perhaps

the most daunting fear of all—the fear of loving themselves first.

THE ULTIMATE REJECTION RISK

I did it on my boyfriend's, Theo's, birthday. We were in a
restaurant surrounded by twenty of our dearest friends,
but it was a struggle to keep myself grounded and to
avoid being engulfed by flashbacks from the past. "Come
on, I can do this" was the mantra I repeated over and over
in my head. "I wasn't supposed to live, but I did. I can do
this." I took a deep breath and patted my pocket; everything was in place. But still, inside, I was so nervous.

Butterflies filled my stomach when I looked around at
everyone. Maybe I shouldn't have invited so many people,
even if they were such good friends. And then I'd start to
worry; how could I overcome my greatest fear, rejection, in
public? Maybe it was expecting too much. The waitress
had just taken the last order and walked away. My stomach turned over. Should I do it now? And then the flashbacks and voices from the past returned. I countered them
inside: "I wasn't supposed to walk, but I did. That was
then; this is now. I can do this." Just when I thought I had
gathered all my courage and was going to do it, another

feeling would overwhelm me. Then I'd say to myself again: "I wasn't supposed to run, but I did. I can do this."

I was eight years old when my life went up in flames. Matches and a gasoline can. The last time I walked or ran without third degree burns covering 90 percent of my body was that night in my bedroom, that night I was trapped by the fire, and I jumped up and down on my bed and screamed for my life. But no one could help me.

I'm an adult now, and it hasn't been easy. The surgeries, the insecurities, the battles, the wounds, the scars. The fear of rejection. Like a room full of flames, feelings from the past would engulf me until I could ground myself in the present: "I've walked through hell, but I've kept on walking. I wasn't supposed to write with two fingers amputated from my right hand, but I did. I can do this. This is now, not then."

I reached into my pocket and pulled out the ring. Then I called out my boyfriend's name. "Theodore Washington." He turned his head and stared at me. It must have been the tone in my voice because everyone at the table got quiet. All eyes were staring at me. In that moment I remembered a friend in high school who, in reference to the scars that cover my skin used to say, "When they stare at you, stare at 'em back! You're a beautiful black girl." With that I took a deep breath—and I did it.

"Theodore Washington . . . will you marry me?"
And he said yes!

Tricia was afraid her boyfriend would reject her proposal of marriage. Ever since she suffered such extensive burns as a child, Tricia has had a fear of not being liked because of the way she looked. As Tricia told us, "I was about eleven years old when I finally got out of the hospital and went back to school. I would always make sure to cover myself at school. Even in the summer I'd be covered from head to toe. I didn't want anyone staring at me. I didn't think anyone would like me." Even though most of us haven't had to contend with such an extreme obstacle as Tricia's injuries, we can identify with her self-consciousness. Whether it was our acne, our weight, or our braces, the fear of being rejected because of our physical appearance can be overwhelming.

When Tricia transcended the fear of rejection and found the courage to propose marriage to her boyfriend, she had no idea that not only would they marry, but they would also have three beautiful children. As Tricia told us, "I really loved Theo, and I wanted to get married. I didn't want our relationship to slip away. But Theo can be very shy, so I decided to try. No matter how many people were staring at me, I just knew I had to try."

◆　　◆　　◆

What can we do when we're faced with the fear of rejection in a relationship? Tom G. Stevens, Ph.D., says, "If your self-image is too closely tied to what others think of you or how well you relate to others, then fear of rejection can be a threat to your whole self-image. That in itself can create a lot of anxiety."[2] The Internet magazine, *Self-Help Psychology*, tells us, "The fear of rejection often lies more in the anticipation than in the actuality. We are more afraid of feelings we imagine we will have than the feelings we actually have . . . Sure, we will feel disappointed, but [rejection] is not devastating unless we allow it to be so. Most of us are quite able to recover from someone saying no. We feel the disappointment or hurt, [and] it passes . . . So, [in] recognizing that we are able to cope with disappointments far better than we think, we can learn to accept rejections and move on."[3]

FEELING SAFE ENOUGH

I remember it vividly. It was a quiet Sunday night. I was with my boyfriend of one year, and our favorite show had just ended. He was getting ready to take me home and I was in his bedroom, collecting my things, when he just came up behind me and grabbed me and started kissing me. He kept kissing and kissing and kissing me, gently backing me up, until my calves were flat against the side of his bed. There was nowhere else to go but down. His arms were clamped around my waist, our chests were pressed tightly together, he had himself braced up over the bed by one knee. He held me securely in his arms and began to bend me backward. I have really long hair and my head was tilted fully back. I remember the way my hair felt when it brushed the mattress, sort of suspended there, before he laid me down flat on the bed. In that moment, I became overwhelmed by passion, passion like I had never experienced before. The sound of his breath in my ear, the feel of his lips on mine, the warmth of his hands as they moved up and down my body. We tore at each other's clothes. I was mentally, physically, and emotionally with him right then, right there, completely focused on the passion of the moment. I felt my body rise in rhythm with

9

his, our hearts beating faster and faster; I was escalating to the point of no return. This was the ultimate, climactic moment—the moment when I always self-sabotaged and pulled back, preventing myself from going over the edge. But that night, the safety I felt allowed the intensity of my feelings to completely wipe out any other thoughts from my head. I surrendered my self-control and let it happen. Finally, I had an orgasm.

Kathryn was afraid to let go of her self-control in a sexual situation. Being raised in an environment where sexual promiscuity was the norm led Kathryn to attach a lot of guilt and shame to the act of sex. "I grew up hearing my mother having orgasms on a regular basis, and I was always afraid of it. It sounded very violent in my child's mind." Because of Kathryn's negative feelings toward sex, she was unable to integrate it with a close relationship. As she told us, "There was never a relationship behind my sexual encounters. They were just one-night stands. There was never trust; there was never knowledge; there was never intimacy."

When Kathryn transcended her fear of losing control in a sexual situation, not only were the benefits immediate, they were also long-term. At last Kathryn was able to talk with her boyfriend about all the shame and guilt she'd attached to sex, and she found he understood. As she told us, "I think the reason I'm able to orgasm with this man is that he loves me, he's patient with me, and he doesn't judge me. He's made our relationship very safe." Kathryn went on to tell us that, while she's able to have an intimate relationship with her boyfriend, she feels a greater sense of intimacy within herself too. "I feel more secure as a human being. I feel loved. I feel lucky. I feel sexy. Having an orgasm has enabled me to accept my body. I even sleep better. I feel very safe."

❖ ❖ ❖

What can we do if we are afraid of sexual intimacy? Although the inability to achieve orgasm doesn't necessarily imply a disorder, Irvin D. Yalom, M.D., of Stanford University, along with Randolph S. Charlton, editors of *Treating Sexual Disorders*, tell us: "Intimacy inherently feels risky because we go out on the edge of individual expression [such as with orgasm] without knowing how the other person will respond."[4] Yalom and Charlton go on to say that an inherent step to the successful treatment of female orgasmic disorder is,

"[The patient] must feel safe and understood [in order to] feel and communicate her sexual desires."[5] Yalom and Charlton also suggest women's sexuality support groups as an effective therapy for female orgasmic disorder. "Women's sexuality groups are recommended for (1) women who have never had an orgasm . . . (2) women with situational arousal and inhibited orgasm, (3) women with uncomplicated vaginismus [a sexual pain disorder], and (4) some women with sexual anxieties either with or without a relationship."[6]

DANCING MY DEFENSES AWAY

I didn't want to go to the dance in the first place. My girlfriend literally had to drag me by the arm. So when this really cute guy started walking across the floor and asked me to dance, I completely shocked myself by saying yes. My mouth just opened up, and out came a word I hadn't said to a man in twelve years. I'd been saying no for so long, and then that night, I said yes to a complete stranger.

So there we were, side by side, walking out to the middle of the dance floor. I looked down every step of the way. My footsteps felt so heavy, burdened with years of resentment, fettered by the betrayal of my ex. Even my shoulders felt heavy, because in my head, men were the enemy, never to be trusted again. It had been so long since I'd been out at all—and even longer since I'd danced.

We reached the middle of the floor, he turned around and smiled at me, and I hesitantly started moving my hips. "This isn't so bad," I thought as I moved my feet back and forth. My arms were swinging, my feet were sliding, the music grew progressively louder. Faster, louder—louder, faster—and then, wham! I just let it rip! The shackles of betrayal and mistrust I carried out to the floor just flew off with every step. I whirled and I twirled as my defenses fell away and my movements became more and more free. The stranger before me was smiling and laughing. He was a man, just a man—not the enemy! I threw my head back and I laughed!

The music was so loud that we couldn't talk, but we danced together like that all night. The minute I opened myself up to life again, life came! He asked for my number when the lights came on, and he called the next day. Six months later he asked me to marry him, and we have been dancing ever since!

Kaye was afraid to trust a man. Because of her first husband's infidelity, as well as his nearly ceaseless verbal abuse, Kaye resisted the possibility of a serious relationship for twelve years. As she told us, "I lost all my trust in men. I didn't want to go through that kind of pain again. That kind of betrayal can hurt so much. It makes you scared to even imagine it happening, much less letting it happen in reality."

When Kaye transcended her fear of trusting men, she found the courage to connect with a man who turned out not only to be her future husband, but also her soul mate. Kaye told us, "Martin and I have such a good time together. We rarely argue, and when we do, we can talk about it. I could never do that with my ex. Martin is supportive, caring, warm, and affectionate. He even makes me coffee in the morning, and rubs the kinks out of my neck. We appreciate each other so much."

◆　　◆　　◆

When we're faced with the fear of being betrayed by a loved one, what can we do? In writing for *salon.com*, psychologist Robert Firestone had some very realistic advice for building a strong, lasting relationship. He said, "[First remember] people have a certain core emptiness that can never be filled by finding another. If we are looking for a person to fill our needs, we're certainly not going to find them. No one can fill a deep emptiness in us. We can never extract from our partners what was missing in our early lives."[7] However, Firestone goes on to say, "There are a number of key characteristics that people should look out for in a potential mate: (1) nondefensiveness, i.e., openness to feedback without reacting with aggression or avoidance; (2) honesty and integrity; (3) respect for the other person's boundaries, priorities and goals; (4) a person who is physically affectionate and comfortable with the sexual role; (5) a person who is empathic and understanding."[8]

LOVE'S SELF-FULFILLING PROPHECY

I had never felt so much anxiety around anything in my life! I became absolutely postal phobic. In the beginning, I would just peek out the window and watch for the mail carrier to come up the driveway. Then as time passed, I actually sat in the house, on the weekends, and waited for the mail truck. I began to listen for, and recognize, the sound of its engine when it turned the corner, all the way down the street. I was so afraid of what might be delivered on any given day that I actually started planning my days around the delivery of the mail. Its schedule became my schedule. I would spend my time pacing and waiting, waiting and pacing. At that point, all I knew was that it would be a disaster if my husband saw the mail first.

But what more could I do?

The day that I looked my fear in the face, I thought I was going to have a nervous breakdown. I'd been waiting for the mail to arrive, and I'd been remembering our wedding. It was awful. I was walking down the aisle on my father's arm, thinking, "I'm twenty-two now. I'll give this man five years, and then I'll be twenty-seven. I'll still have time to find someone I really want to be with, and have children with, before I turn thirty." Can you imagine thinking such thoughts on your wedding day? Well, guess what? It was a self-fulfilling prophecy because almost exactly five years after our marriage, I filled out and mailed the paperwork for a simple, no-attorneys-involved divorce.

After five years, our marriage was over. But then, while we were apart, something happened. I mean, during the separation, we worked really hard on ourselves. We both got sober. We let go of the past and began to rebuild trust. We'd both been so afraid to feel . . . to feel emotional intimacy. We used to drink it away, but not anymore. While we were apart, we both changed.

So on the day I faced my fear I was waiting for the mail, doing my pacing—the whole thing—when suddenly, it just hits me. I don't want my husband to see the divorce papers because . . . I still love him! It was like I couldn't really admit it to myself until that moment—because that is my greatest fear: to love someone and to be loved by someone. So the fact is, I really didn't want a divorce! I finally had the man I wanted. And he was my husband all along. It really hit me! I love my husband. But I also knew that if he saw the divorce papers in the mail first, it could put a knife in the heart of our relationship.

What could I do?! Those papers were in the mail!

God must have heard me that day; something was protecting us. Because those final papers to the divorce decree, they never came through. Somehow they just never came. And so my husband never knew.

Jewel was afraid both of giving and of receiving love. When Jewel's parents emigrated from the Dominican Republic to New York City, they had to work very hard to make ends meet, and consequently, they were rarely home during Jewel's formative years. When Jewel was five, her parents divorced, and her mother was even busier trying to support the family. As Jewel told us, "To this day, my mother does not hug very well; my mother does not kiss very well. Her demeanor is to push you away. Most of my family is like that. They just don't know how to express affection for each other. But I always had a yearning for affection, and the idea of never having that yearning fulfilled really scared me." Because Jewel feared emotional neglect, she turned to alcohol, which numbed those feelings.

In transcending her fear of giving and receiving love, Jewel's life is in full and fantastic bloom. Jewel and her husband both attended a twelve-step program where they discovered the fear behind their alcohol abuse and learned about family dysfunction. She told us, "I don't have to live in fear now. I was able to realize that I don't have to be my mother. I am in a place now where I can love my mom for who she is. I appreciate her for the things she did right and learn from what she did wrong. I am open with love and can receive love, and I've been happily married for sixteen years." Jewel and her husband also have a child, and Jewel has recently graduated from school to become an acupuncturist.

❖   ❖   ❖

There are many centers that teach the twelve-step program. They can be found from coast to coast in rural neighborhoods and large cities. Dial 411 and ask for Alcoholics Anonymous for a phone number to call in your area. AA volunteers will provide you with times, days, and locations of the nearest meetings in your area. Alternatives to the twelve-step approach, including addiction services, inpatient and outpatient treatment centers, and crisis hotlines, can be found in the Information Guide located in the front your phone book.

AFRAID TO CHOOSE

I think again, like I've thought too many times to count, "How can I build my happiness on someone else's pain?" My father's pain. My father, whom I love and cherish and would do anything for, but can I do this? Can I give up Cliff? My one true love? Oh, why must I say goodbye to one or the other? Why must I choose? My eyes fill with tears, and I turn my face to the window. I can't allow my sorrow to spill; it's like blood. It's like . . . family. I feel like I'm killing someone. I can't choose. I wipe at my eyes. Who will it be?

My parents are in the front seat of the car; no one's talking. I remember hundreds of times being in the car with my mother and father, having so much to say to each other. So much to explore, and laugh about, and learn; it's always been that way with my parents. Always, until these days—these torturous days. That's what I feel like I'm doing. I'm torturing my father, punishing him—and hasn't he been punished enough? Didn't he lose so many loved ones to the Holocaust? But didn't Cliff lose as many ancestors to the slave ships and the hanging trees? Haven't we all paid enough? Why should we cultivate more hate among us when we haven't even come to terms with the hate that remains? I am Jewish. Cliff is black. We are in love. We are, all of us, in pain. My father clears his throat.

"Marly," he says, "will you come to our New Year's Eve party? Will you, please?"

My mother smiles at me, then winces and looks away. I know how important this event is to my parents, how rare it is that they would give such a party, and how big it will be, full of family, and laughter, and the kind of love that only comes from joy, and tears, and life. I want to have a life! I have never missed an event like this; I love my family. It has been my mantra—I love my family. But, I love

Cliff. My father will never invite him to this gathering. My father will not even consent to meet him!

It almost erupts from my lips. "No, I can't make it, Dad." I hear his sharp intake of breath; he can't believe it. I've always been there, but not this time. How can I try to please him when he's not even willing to meet me halfway? I say again, "No, Dad."

I have chosen.

Marly was afraid that she wouldn't be able to choose between her father and the love of her life. Like Marly, many women have had to choose between family and falling in love with a person of another race, ethnicity, or culture, and there can be a great deal of fear involved with such a decision. As Marly told us, "My father had formed an opinion, and his bias was considerable. But I love my father, so I tried to honor his wishes, and I refused to go out with Cliff for more than two years. Then when I finally did go out with Cliff, I was sure I'd never go out with him again. Instead, I spent two more years trying to break up with him, but love kept bringing me back, over and over—I couldn't leave him. Still, every time Cliff would ask me to marry him, I'd say no. I was so afraid to hurt my father."

In transcending her fear of making a choice between the two men she loved most, Marly felt an immediate and overwhelming sense of satisfaction. She told us, "When I turned down the invitation to one of the biggest events in my parent's life, I knew I'd made a choice in favor of Cliff, but then my father took me by complete surprise. He kept his eyes focused on the road, but his voice was almost quivering when he said, 'Will you be able to come if we invite him?' Him—meaning Cliff. I started sobbing, and all of a sudden it was like the floodgates had been opened, and we all—my father, my mother, and I—started talking at once. We talked about everything, everything we'd avoided for two years." But the best was yet to come. Marly said, "Cliff came to the New Year's Eve party, and my family—my parents, my siblings, my aunts and uncles, my cousins, everyone—met him and embraced him. And right after the party, literally right after, Cliff asked me to marry him, and I finally was able to say, freely and openly, yes!" Marly and Cliff have been happily married for fifteen years, and they have two beautiful daughters.

◆　　◆　　◆

What can we do when faced with the fear of choosing a mate who is different from what others expect? In America, there is more and more evidence of tolerance for interracial couples. In a recent *Washington Post* article, it was reported that "Since 1960 the number of interracial couples has increased more than tenfold, to 1.6 million . . . and that is already offering powerful evidence that many Americans are jettisoning old prejudices as never before."[9] In the same article, Reynolds Farley, a demographer with the *Russell Sage Foundation*, stated, "I think we are at the edge of a major change in how we think of race in the United States. Potentially, race could lose much of its meaning in this country, much like ethnicity has for whites."[10]

SELF-ACCEPTANCE

Shafts of light from the afternoon sun are shining through the bedroom window. We have just finished making love, and you have gotten up and are walking through a beam of light. I am lying in bed watching this with the sounds of suburbia all around me, when out of nowhere, I am overwhelmed with hideous self-loathing. I close my eyes, but I can't get rid of it. I hate who I am, and

I hate what I'm doing. I hate me; I hate you; I hate this. I rock and I rock and I rock back and forth, holding my arms across my stomach. I try to hold down my revulsion, but I think I'm going to be sick. Pounding my fist into the mattress I get angry, and as I do, I lift my head and look to the left. I see our cat curled up on the chair, sleeping peacefully, clear across the room. I look straight ahead out the window to the cars parked on the street, and become aware of a dog barking next door. A tidal wave of disgust sweeps over me. Again I begin to rock.

I rock and rock to the rhythm of the music that I left behind so long ago. Has it already been a year? Strobe lights flash in my mind while bodies writhe on the dance floor. People pass by me, setting their drinks on the bar. They are leaving the club life behind them as they head out the door.

Now I'm back in our bedroom, looking around, surrounded by suburbia once more. I am repulsed by the inescapable fact that this is my reality, not some fantasy nightclub scene. When I go out today and close the door behind me, it is the same door I will come home through tonight. And it will be the same every day. I have no distraction of music and strobe lights; I have no ability to leave! I am not a traditional woman, but we have been leading a traditional life. And that's why I'm so afraid. My moment of truth has arrived. This is the fact from which I can no longer run: You are my lover, my significant other. You are a woman. And I have just made the decision to lead the rest of my life—as a lesbian.

Eve was afraid to confront the reality of her sexual orientation. She told us, "As long as I was staying out late going to nightclubs and leading a kind of 'unreal' lifestyle, my lesbianism could still seem kind of unreal. But in my late twenties, I began living with a woman in a very traditional type of situation. It became harder and harder for me to deny the reality of my lesbian status to myself. Then one day, right after we'd made love, it just hit me, and all my homophobic fears came rushing in. I hated myself. Really hated myself. It was terrible."

In order to transcend her fear, Eve had to find the courage to face it, which she did. That fateful afternoon, Eve realized that being a lesbian did not mean she had to visualize herself as an unreal party person, but rather, recognize that she was a stable, traditional, highly ethical human being. Over a decade has passed since that day, and Eve has been in a monogamous relationship for many years. She told us, "Ever since I came to that decision inside myself, I have searched for relationships of true substance and meaning. I really value high moral standards and decency. I know that might sound incongruous to some—because my sexual preference is often considered immoral—but it is the way I've chosen to live my life. I am very traditional, but I am also a lesbian."

◆　　◆　　◆

Violence and harassment against the lesbian and gay community is real. Here are some safety tips from the *Anti-Violence Project* (AVP) that may help reduce your risk of possible danger: (1) Stay alert. Awareness is your best defense. (2) Trust your instincts. Don't assume a false sense of security because you are either surrounded by people or in a remote area. (3) Evaluate and be aware of your surroundings. Use well-lit, busy streets. (4) Carry a whistle. If you feel threatened, blow your whistle, bang garbage cans, honk your horn, or shout to attract attention. (5) Do not open your door to strangers without verifying their identity. (6) Report all incidents of violence or harassment; that's the only way it can be stopped from happening again.[11]

THE PRICE OF LOVE

I am sitting in a room with the ocean at my back, watching the five couples we are traveling with and observing how happy they are. They are suited mates, clearly in love, enjoying coupledom. And here you are, my potential husband-to-be, sitting next to me on the couch. I know you are waiting for an answer, and the anticipation of it is making me sick. You reach out and touch my shoulder. I look down at the diamond watch adorning my wrist and smile sadly. I look beyond you to the wall—and years and years beyond. And I wonder, when did I first sell out?

"Will you marry me? Yes or no?"

All week long, you have showered me with expensive gifts while you patiently wait for my answer. I'm aware of the distance growing between us although you have not moved away an inch. I continue to watch the people in this room. I hear their murmurs and giggles around me, the sound of champagne pouring into crystal flutes. As I watch the bubbles rise to the top, I wonder, why do I feel so low? Somewhere in the shadow side of my mind lurks the question I am most afraid to answer. Does the price of my independence come down to this, a luxurious lifestyle? It hasn't fixed anything yet.

I turn my head and look over my shoulder, out to the far-reaching sea. I have traveled the oceans and slept with princes and kings. What has that gotten me? Baubles and jewels; but not self-esteem. Looking up to the sky, I see a plane passing by. I've flown around the world on private jets, yet never felt more alone. I've been catered to and pampered like a queen, and now here I am, doing what? Giving in to my fears and giving up on my dreams.

The fear in my heart tells me that if I marry you, I'm settling for less than I deserve. I'll be striking a bargain in which I am the trump card, cheating myself in a lifelong deal. Tilting my head to the side, I pinch the diamond in my ear. Fully despising myself, I know I'm worthy of more. I'm worthy of real, deep-seated, wonderful, turn-your-world-upside-down love. I don't love you like that, and I know I never will.

I excuse myself and escape to the privacy of an empty bathroom. I close the door behind me and look at myself in the mirror. The realization of a lifetime occurs to me in the flash of this one second. I'm a thirty-nine-year-old woman who has just learned a lesson. All my life someone else has paid my way because I've been afraid that I can't take care of myself. My greatest fear is financial independence. With this thought comes my next realization: love is not the price of a ring, nor is independence about things. In this moment of clarity I know that I would rather be alone and live like a pauper than be chained like a prisoner to fear. I will know love, and I will take responsibility for myself! My own fear has come with the highest price tag of all, and it's called self-esteem.

"No. I will not marry you." Now I am finally free.

Because Reisa was raised in an environment where money was scarce, she grew up with a fear of never being able to support herself financially. Reisa's father also had a devastating effect on her self-esteem. As she told us, "He would repeatedly tell me I needed to marry someone to take care of me because I'd never be able to take care of myself. So I grew up with a huge fear that I'd never be able to provide for myself, and I spent most of my adult life dating powerful, rich men who paid my rent or gave me expensive gifts. I truly felt that if I was left to provide for myself, something terrible would happen. I would end up starving, or even dead!"

When Reisa transcended her fear of not being able to support herself financially, she found the courage to turn down a proposal of marriage from a wealthy man whom she didn't love. She began to feel very differently about herself. She told us, "There's a sense of pride. There's a security in being on my own that I've never experienced before because it's coming from within. I used to have to know what the other person was thinking, what they were doing. I never trusted any of the men I was with. But what I really needed was to learn how to trust myself." Reisa has become financially independent, working as a fitness instructor, and is pursuing a master's degree in east/west psychology. Her goal is to become a spiritual counselor. She now feels secure enough about herself to know that if she ever does marry, it need not be for financial support, but for love.

❖　　❖　　❖

When we are afraid of independence, we may be experiencing codependence. Melody Beattie writes in her best-selling book, *Beyond Codependency:* "Many good definitions of codependency have surfaced . . . [several are] . . . 'a set of maladaptive, compulsive behaviors learned by family members to survive in a family experiencing great emotional pain and stress . . . Behaviors . . . passed on from generation to generation whether alcoholism is present or not.'" Beattie goes on to say, "Codependency [can also appear as] . . . a person who has let someone else's behavior affect him or her, and is obsessed with controlling other people's behavior."[12]

Beattie suggests there *is* recovery from codependency: "Instead of obsessively trying to control others, we learn to detach. Instead of allowing others to hurt and use us, we set boundaries. Instead of reacting, we learn to relax and let things settle into place. We replace tunnel vision with perspective. We forego worrying and denial, and learn constructive problem-solving skills. We learn to feel and express feelings; we learn to value what we want and need; we stop punishing ourselves for other people's problems, nonsense and insanity . . . We learn to function in relationships. We learn to love ourselves, so we can better love others."[13]

LEAVING THE BAD BOYS BEHIND

I was so attracted to him. He was just the kind of man I always fell for, a bad boy charmer. He had that spark in his eyes that spelled trouble, and I liked trouble. Loved trouble. It turned me on, mostly because I understood it. So the Man That Was Trouble looks at me, smiling his charming smile. I've been seeing him for a while, and I know he's been cheating on me. What man who's trouble doesn't end up doing that, huh? He's been cheating on me, and I know it like I know my own face in the mirror. My own face that's got a big scar running across the top of my head, right here, under my hair. I got this scar falling off a bike. I hit my head on the pavement and almost died. Seems innocent enough, right? But I'd been partying all night, and when morning came, my girlfriend and I decided to go bike riding.

Can you believe that?

The doctors were sure I was going to die. I had to have brain surgery, and I probably would have died but for my daddy. That's what I believe. He came to see me on that operating table. He was dead as can be, but he was there, and he wanted to help me. I could feel that. I could see him right next to me, and feel his spirit helping me. Helping me, like he never could when he was alive. It was the booze that killed him, just like it almost killed me.

I forgave my daddy that day, and I lived.

I think I even forgave myself. A child can't carry the world on her shoulders. A child can't be responsible for a parent's alcoholism. A child just can't be made to feel that bad.

So why am I with this bad boy?! Why?!

I'm at this fancy restaurant with the best-looking bad boy charmer I've ever dated, and he's cheating on me, and

I know, but like always, I'm not going to confront him, am I? I'm not going to challenge him. I'm not going to look him in the eye and make him tell me the truth, because, because, I'm afraid to! Without this familiar brand of evil, what do I have? He turns and gives the waitress a grin, I can tell she likes it, and he swings back to me, so smooth, the lies spilling from his tongue like Sunday school prayers—he's just that damn graceful! He's just that damn cute! He's just that damn bad.

I stand up, slowly, and he says, "Where ya goin', darlin'? Come on back here. Come on, darlin.'" And I say, "Find someone else to mess with because you're not messin' with me anymore!"

Julie was afraid she wouldn't be able to walk away from a bad relationship and make a commitment to herself. She grew up feeling on the one hand betrayed by her alcoholic father and, on the other hand, somehow responsible for her father's alcoholism and subsequent death. As Julie told us, "I had a lot of guilt and shame and by the time I hit my twenties, I was pursuing a very dangerous path. It was always party, party, party. I couldn't keep jobs very long or relationships. I was constantly craving excitement, and I would always get serious about men who were equally destructive."

When Julie transcended her fear of making a commitment to herself, she found the courage to change her life. As she told us, "I started making all sorts of commitments to myself. Instead of beating myself up about falling for yet another bad boy, I put together a résumé, got a job as a cosmetologist, and started taking really good care of myself—something I'd never done before. And then I met my husband, Larry." When we asked Julie what made Larry different from the destructive types that she'd been attracted to before, she replied, "He's such a sweet guy. He's the kind of guy I could never have been with before. His sweetness would have scared me. His commitment to me would have frightened me because I couldn't commit to myself." Just six months after they met, Julie and Larry were married, and now they have two children. As Julie said, "We're very happy."

◆　◆　◆

Adult Children of Alcoholics World Service (ACA) suggests that when we release our parents from the responsibility for our actions today, we become free to make healthful decisions. They also say that when we take responsibility for our own life, we begin to supply our own parenting. In essence, we become our own loving parent. ACA suggests using the twelve-steps to recover the child within you and learn to love and accept yourself.[14]

Choosing Love

Love is a blessing. To feel love, for all its folly and fearsome curves, is to also feel close to our idea of heaven, even God. After all, it is in love's beneficent arms that we can surrender both our tragedies and everyday travails. We love to be loved, and to live without love can sometimes feel as if we're living without air. As human beings, we seek the warm, generous spirit of love, and without it we may risk our own emotional, if not physical, well-being.

The arranged marriage has gone the way of the horse-and-buggy. Today we are making our own decisions. Do I love you? Will I marry you? Yes, no, maybe. It is our prerogative to choose, but with it comes a great responsibility. We direct our own destiny and while that can, at times, be frightening, we also know it is a right we would defend over and over again.

As we enter this new century, we have more opportunity than ever before to find and keep true love. In an interview for *Psychology Today,* John Gray, Ph.D., author of *Men Are From Mars, Women Are From Venus*, said: "Before 1950, everybody knew . . . men were men and women were women. There was 'men's work' and there was 'women's work' . . . We were really in separate worlds. What's happening today is a huge transformation. It's the possibility of something greater than has ever happened before for relationships. Romeo and Juliet fell in love, and the only reason their love is eternal is because they died. If they had gotten married, their love would not have lasted. Never before in recorded history did people marry and have lasting romance and passion. [But now] When women cross over into the man's world, the two worlds come together. And there can be friction or there can be harmony."[15]

It is our choice.

In recent years, society has been striving to treat women and men in an equal manner, and this equality lets us decide just how we want to live with each other. At this new juncture, if we are receptive, the possibilities are endless. Marianne Williamson, author of *A Return to Love*, says, "We are not held back by the love we didn't receive in the past, but by the love we're not extending in the present."[16]

Women will continue to choose love for it is our natural forte as sensitive, empathic, nurturing beings, as well as something we desire. We not only *embody* love, but we can now make a conscious choice to reach out with open arms and embrace it.

Courage and Success

*Why Are Women Afraid of
Their Own Potential?*

For our voice will be heard,
louder and louder, as we continue
to challenge the status quo and defend
ourselves against those who would
usurp our freedom.

WHAT KIND OF FEAR does success evoke in women? And if we fear success, is it our own fear, or was it ingrained in us by a societal pressure that has been passed down for ages? Throughout much of history, many women who sought success or the power to control their own destiny were ostracized, or worse. We have only to look to the story of Joan of Arc, who in 1429 led her troops to win battle after battle for the French over England, but as Gloria Steinem said, "Once the wars were won, [Joan of Arc] had too much power and so she had to be burned as a witch."[1] Success, power, autonomy—those were the strongholds of the male domain, and to breach those strongholds could be a very frightening, if not fatal, undertaking.

But how do we feel about success now?

Do we still fear it? Or have we transcended the threat of ostracism and fiery punishment? More women flank the hallowed halls of the justice department, congress, and the senate than ever before. We are doctors, scientists, professors, executives, journalists, and astronauts. We have clout in every arena because we are a huge voting block and we have money, our own hard-earned money. In 1948, Charlotte Woodward campaigned to change laws that gave husbands the right to pocket their wives' earnings.[2] Now we can buy our own home, our own business, our own vacation paradise. It is our right and a right we continue to defend.

In this chapter we will meet women who have acknowledged a fear of success and conquered it with intellect, fortitude, and dignity. They have met the challenge of resistance head on, and left all opposition to shame. They are our champions. They are our valedictorians. They are all of us. Working, learning, growing, and getting there—inch by inch if that's what it takes. They have culled the light from fear and left behind its darkness. They hail us toward each new day.

I Will Be Seen

Before I'm even out of bed, already I feel slightly ill. I wonder what resentment I will encounter at work today? As always I know the guys will be sneering when I walk into the plant. I shuffle to the kitchen to make my coffee knowing that I cannot give in to their pressure. I must go in and I must go on. I'm only eighteen years old, but mine is a heavy load. I awaken my child with a kiss and a hug, and as I do, I silently pray he will not encounter in his life what I will face at work today. As I take my morning shower, an intuitive feeling washes over me with a chill; today is going to be even worse than usual. But I must go on and I must go in. An hour later as I drop my baby off, I murmur into his ear, "You can do anything you want. Never give up and never give in. Make them see you."

I drive to the plant feeling nervous. No one speaks to me as I walk in. One by one the men turn away. I punch the time clock and take a deep breath. What difficulties do they have in store for me today? I reach my locker and pull out my toolbox. The men are all staring at me now waiting for my response as I see the nudie pictures they have taped to it, yet again. And as an additional touch, today they have glued it shut. I will not struggle. I will not cry. I will not react to them at all. I hear them chuckle. They sneer and turn away.

The foreman is shouting my last name and shaking his finger across the room. I follow the direction of his hand with my eyes. It's another machine in this industrial plant. It's so loud in here that I can't hear what he's shouting, but I walk over to the machine. He nods, yes, yes. This particular machine looks like some kind of fuel tank. He wants me to work on it today, but no one has, or will, show me how. And so I reach up, I pull the lever down, and I begin to scream.

Something has exploded! I hear it and smell it; it has blown up on me! I begin to run, hysterically, screaming! My head is on fire! I cannot think and I cannot see! Flames have engulfed my head! My hair is on fire! The smell of burning skin, the smell of burning hair! I scream and yell and run, with no idea of where I'm going. Someone puts out the fire that has devoured my head, and I fade away into black.

I awaken in the hospital, and eventually I can return to my home. Weeks pass until the day I have been dreading most arrives, the day I have to go back to the plant. The time has come to face them again, but I must go on and I must go in. I cannot give in to my fears. They will see me. I will make them see me. They will see that I am still alive.

I begin my drive to the plant, and as I do I begin to feel queasy. The disgust that the men openly display toward me hurts more than these burns on my skin. I park. I walk. I punch in. My hair is burned off, my head is bald, my nose is still covered in bandages. I maintain my composure, but this is almost too much. I must continue to put one foot in front of the other, take it one day, one step at a time.

It is unusually quiet in the plant I notice as I approach my locker door. I take a deep breath and reach in for my

toolbox. No nudie pictures today. I heave a little sigh and
. . . did I just hear someone call my first name? No, it's not
possible. "Good morning," I did hear someone say.
Turning to look over my shoulder, I see all the men standing, looking at me. There is no sneering today. One man
lifts his hand in a gesture of hello. He looks ashamed. Now
he looks away. From across the building the foreman walks
and extends to me, the only black female in an all-white
plant, a cup of coffee.

I've been seen. At last, I've been seen.

Michele was afraid that, because of racial discrimination, she would be unable to make enough money to go
to college and follow her dreams. Michele told us,
"When the tank at the plant exploded on me, I thought
I might never be able to leave my house, let alone go to
college. I was aware that those guys at the plant didn't
want me there. They didn't want to work with me. I was
the first black woman and the first black person to ever
work with those guys, and they'd been there forever.
Did they cause the accident? Not really, but they never
taught me about the tank either. The bottom line is it
shouldn't have happened. Not under any circumstance."

When Michele transcended her fear of being discriminated against, she found the courage to go back to work and earn the money she needed for college. Michele is the first black woman with her own real estate business in the prime area of West Los Angeles. She also has properties in Northern California and New York. Michele told us, "I try to find my clients the home of their dreams. That's what has really led to my success. Everyone has a dream home, and I just keep looking and looking until I find it." In fact, that kind of tenacity could be Michele's motto for living. "As a black woman, I have always put myself in positions where I was the first, and the way I did that was that I've never been afraid to work hard, and I don't give up. See, people will put this block in my face or not listen to me, and I kind of wave and say, I'm still here. I learned that at the plant a long time ago. I just keep staying—and eventually, people come around."

◆　　◆　　◆

What can we do when faced with the fear of racial discrimination? For black women in business, the twenty-first century appears to be looking brighter. In an article for *Black Enterprise,* author Robyn D. Clarke wrote,

"For example, fifteen firms run by [black women] are among the top companies recognized by *Black Enterprise.* Five made the Industrial Service 100 list, six made the Financial 50 list, two the Advertising list, and two the Auto Dealer 100 list . . . [Like] Ann Fudge, the first African-American woman to head a division of a Fortune 500 company, black women have also demonstrated that they mean business. [Black women] owned businesses employ more than a quarter of a million people [and] generate over $24.7 billion in annual sales."[3] The article goes on to report A. Lorraine Jones, Atlantic regional director of the National Association of Women Business Owners (NAWBO), as saying, "Black women are awakening to the fact that we really can pursue 'the dream' through business ownership."[4]

"JUST A GIRL"

"Mom?" I said into the phone. "Mom? It's Cynthia . . ." I heard my mother gasp. "Mom." I hadn't spoken to either of my parents in years. My heart was pounding. Did I really want to do this?

I had just graduated premed with a 3.9 grade average. I was on my way to being a doctor. I'm gifted, and ethical, and a valuable member of my community. I've conquered everything I've wanted to do. So far.

But making that phone call was something I didn't think I could do. Because, if I did, what would I become? What would happen to me?

My mother hung on the phone. "Cynthia? Cynthia? Is that you?"

But it was my father's voice I was hearing, weaving around me from years ago. "Sure, you've got some smarts," he said, while leaning against that old, splintery fence. "Sure you do," he said again, with a shake of his head. "But you're just a girl."

I grew up on a farm in small-town Minnesota, and my brothers were considered the truly smart ones. My brothers were the ones my father trusted and pushed. It wasn't fair! I had ambition too. I had dreams. I had strengths. But nobody saw it. In their eyes, I would always be "just a girl."

"Cynthia?" My mother breathed again. "Are you still there? Cynthia?" I could tell her voice was older. More fragile. Could I do this? Did I want to do this? Did I really?

When I told my mother and father that I wanted to go to medical school, you know what they said to me? "How can you do that, dear? You're not scientifically oriented." That hurt more than anything I've ever had to withstand. It hurt more than all the sexual intimidation I've ever experienced as a woman seeking a job in a man's profession. It hurt more than if someone had taken an ice pick to my heart. I was devalued, demoted, almost destroyed, right then and there by my own flesh and blood. My own parents! But I survived. I worked my way through Colombia premed—taking care of other people's children, waitressing, I did it. Me. The girl. The non-scientifically oriented just-a-girl girl. But could I do this?

"Cynthia?" My mother's voice was becoming frightened. "Cynthia?! Are you there?!" It had been so long, so long to hold this kind of anger. This kind of fear. Fear that if I forgave them, I wouldn't be as strong as I needed to be to keep making it in this field.

"Mom," I said, struggling to keep my voice in control. "Mom, I'm married, I have a three-month-old son, and I just got accepted to medical school." My voice cracked. "Mom, I'd like to see you."

Cynthia was afraid that seeing her parents again would make her feel vulnerable and that she would end up a failure. As Cynthia told us, "I suppose my father's attitude wasn't all that unusual for his generation, but the 'just a girl' comment hurt so much. It made me feel so insignificant and weak. I wanted him to be proud of me, but it always seemed like he really couldn't be proud of me. As a girl, I would never truly measure up."

In transcending her fear of failure, Cynthia was able to reconnect with her parents which, in turn, gave her more courage than ever to excel at her chosen profession. Cynthia told us, "I used to feel a lot of pressure to please my father, even if I wasn't in touch with him. Feeling that pressure would make me feel worthless. It would feel as if I placed no value on my own opinion of myself. But after I'd made contact again with my family, I noticed that the pressure and the subsequent insecurity I'd carried around for such a long time had begun to subside. I realized I was no longer reliant on my father's opinion. I'd faced him and maintained my personal integrity. I knew, right then, that I was strong enough to succeed at anything." Dr. Cynthia A. Boxrud has advanced to ever-greater stature within the medical ranks. She is an ophthalmic facial plastic reconstructive surgeon as well as a cosmetic surgeon. She went to medical school at Case Western Reserve in Cleveland, Ohio, and trained at NYU and Bellevue. She was a fellow at Cornell and is still on staff. Cynthia has been quoted in a number of magazines and has a thriving practice in southern California.

◆ ◆ ◆

As women, how can we transcend the fear of failure in our careers? In an article for *careerlab.com,* we found several methods to help us overcome our job insecurities, such as: "Your mind is your obedient servant. It will do anything you want. Ask it for a list of ten positive things you can do right now to stop the fear. Write them down—and do them . . . Be willing to accept 'No's. No doesn't mean 'never.' It may mean, 'Not now, maybe later.' It can also mean, 'You don't belong here. There's a better place for you somewhere.' Most important of all: Understand that the universe is incomplete without you (that's why you're here). Because of your life experience you have skills, ideas, and feelings to contribute that no one else can ever match. Why let fear stop you from having your brightest dreams?"[5]

COUNTDOWN TO SUCCESS

"Three . . ."

I'm not in elementary school anymore. I can do this. I was a good student. I was! Except when it came to this, but that's all over now. I'm a grown woman. And I'm not panicking! It's too late for excuses, besides, I can't get out of it now. It's my job! Therefore, it stands to reason that if I'm good enough to be paid for this, then I'm good enough to . . . but they don't know it's my first time!

"Two . . ."

Oh, my God! I can! I can't! I have to! Images of being humiliated in public are flashing through my head. I remember fifteen years ago, when I was reading in public, someone actually shouting from across the room, "What are you, some kind of idiot?" From that day forward I promised myself I would *never* do this again! Now I have one second to get a grip or everything I've worked so hard for is gone.

"One . . ."

I will not allow my fears to control my life! I am not going to let my fears hold me back anymore. They don't know that this is my greatest fear because I'm smiling, I'm taking a deep breath, and . . .

"And we're rolling."

"Hello. I'm Maryanne, and this is the *Channel Twelve Evening News.*"

Maryanne was afraid that she would never be able to read out loud in public. "It started when I was young. I was good in school, but I never could read out loud easily. I always felt insecure when I read in public. Everyone had always told me I should be a news broadcaster because I liked it and because I'm great at public speaking, as long as I don't have to read. I couldn't even read a story to the kids I baby-sat. So I kept putting off my dream of being a broadcaster due to fear and not being willing to take the chance."

When Maryanne Elliott transcended her fear of reading in public, her career was immediately transported to a higher level. She found the courage to attain a job as a TV journalist for CBS, and she is living her life to the fullest, with no regrets. As Maryanne told us, "I have always been driven by a burning desire to have no regrets. And that is part of my being able to overcome my fear. It's easy to be safe and go along with the status quo because of fear, but I don't want to look back and think, 'I could have done that, but I was too afraid.' What I most wanted, I was most afraid of. But I did it. And I have this sense of completion and joy in knowing that anything is possible."

◆   ◆   ◆

What can we do when confronted with the fear of humiliating ourselves in public? There are a variety of techniques that can help us overcome the fear of public speaking. The *anxietycoach.com* suggests: "People need to *practice* what scares them in order to get over their fear. That's desensitization. This doesn't mean you have to start giving long speeches right away, but it does mean that recovery will be accomplished by working *with* your fear, not by resisting it . . ." One good place to get such practice is at a local Toastmasters Club. Toastmasters is an international organization devoted to helping people become better public speakers.[6]

MAKING ENEMIES, LOSING FRIENDS

I sat there thinking, "What's wrong with this picture?" I'm in a courtroom. I'm in a suit. I look like I fit in. I've always fit in. I never wanted to be perceived as different. But now I am. These men in front of me, some of them could be the fathers of kids I went to high school with. Friends. It's so easy when you're a kid. Whatever Karen's dad does, doesn't matter, just as long as Karen is nice, and you have fun, and she lives in a big house on top of a hill. You don't ask why she lives in a big house. You just know that both your parents approve of your friendship, and that makes you feel good.

I look around—lots of faces. These are people I know; I know them as sure as if I'd grown up with each and every one of them. They are rich. They are educated. They are old money. They ski Vail or Aspen in the winter, sail Maine or Nantucket in the summer, throw fantastic parties, and have zillions of dollars, but they usually drive Volvos—so as not to show it off too much. They don't need to show it off. They are that rich. And here I am to testify against them. I'm here to testify about the dangers of nuclear waste. I have to focus my nervousness. I know I'm here to save lives. But I feel like I'm betraying my childhood. I feel ashamed. How could that be? These people have tens of thousands of tons of nuclear waste, and they argue it has to go somewhere. But where should it go? These same people will make tens of millions of dollars building a nuclear waste site. But should it go here? This is home to over a million American citizens. This is a home to several Indian reservations. This is home to a major river. This is home to thousands of species.

They're looking at me. They're ready for my testimony.

I've graduated with honors from one of the finest colleges, worked in Washington, D.C., put in hundreds of hours of research, and I suddenly feel like a fool. My heart is pounding like a hammer. My head feels light. Who am I? Really? Who am I to know what is right to do and what is wrong? I look out across the courtroom and see a little girl clutching her mother's hand. She is about ten years old. Everyone knows it by now: nuclear waste is not good for our children. Nuclear waste is not good for our health.

So that's what it comes down to. After all the tests, the debate, the documentation, I know what everybody else knows—rich or poor, whatever color, whatever friends will still like me, and whatever friends won't. It's common sense, that's what gets me over my fear. And that's what I say to my first committee. "I wouldn't want to live next to a nuclear waste dump. Would you?"

Wendy was afraid that she would lose her friends if she took an environmental stand against them or the industries they were involved in. Wendy told us, "I grew up in a fairly affluent, upper middle-class family. My peers were from the wealthiest families. I had always tried to fit in. I'd always had a huge fear of bucking the system, maybe because my older sister was a rebel, so I tried to be the proper one. I was going to do the easy thing, go to law school and get a degree and start making a lot of money and be a success. I didn't ever think I'd go against the system. But deep down, maybe I had a greater fear of injustice."

When Wendy transcended the fear of losing her friends in favor of supporting something she felt a particular passion for, she found her life became that much more rewarding. As she told us, "I found new friends that shared my same values, and I found out some old friends did too." Wendy Wendlandt is the National Political Director for all of the State PIRGs, and Associate Director for CalPIRG. Each PIRG is a nonprofit public interest research group designed to inform and assist citizens in social, environmental, and political awareness. Wendy went on to say, "I can't save the world. But I can save a piece of it. I'm like a person driving down the road, and I see there is a problem, and I stop and try to help. To me, it's as simple as that. And the more you know, the more imperative it is you stop. Say you're a doctor, then you definitely have to stop. In my case, I've learned skills that allow me to stop and do something, help someone. Listen, we got rid of CFCs (chlorofluorocarbons), and that seemed futile. But we realized they were bad for the environment, for the ozone, and we got rid of them. So maybe it's not futile. The ultimate goal is to try. Just get people to try."

* * *

What can we do when faced with a fear of losing our peers to our passions? In terms of the environment, women have played an ever-larger role in making a once unpopular issue like ecology popular. Shannon Cunnif, a senior policy analyst since 1994 for the Department of the Interior and the Environmental Protection Agency, writes: "It was the contributions of—and publicity given to—scientists like Dian Fossey and Jane Goodall . . . that showed the world that women were equally equipped for . . . [leading] new avenues of [environmental] exploration. These women who chose to think and act 'outside the box,' inspired me. They were pioneers and role models. They lived their dreams undaunted by criticism, cronyism, and setbacks. They enriched the world by being here."[7]

An Aid to Introspection

I'm lying there thinking, "Let me up! I don't have time to be strapped to this board!" But my greatest fear was beginning to creep up on me.

I had just turned forty when I decided to go back to school, to get my doctoral degree in homeopathy. Boom! Next thing, I get into an automobile accident. Not just any accident, an accident with a seriously high profile attorney's son who refuses to cooperate, so I have to hire a lawyer of my own. While I'm laid up recovering, the school informs me that unless I complete a dissertation within a limited amount of time I won't qualify for their doctoral degree. In no way am I prepared to begin a dissertation—on what? But I have to begin or I lose everything!

A few weeks pass. Now I'm facing possible bankruptcy from medical and legal bills because of the accident when I get into accident number two! I get rear ended while sitting at a stoplight. Accident number two sends me to the hospital with whiplash, where I am strapped to a board all day, being seen by neurologists. And I am completely alone during all of this, with no one to call. No friends, no relationships. Because, you see, I had withdrawn and become isolated, because of the dissertation, and school, and the first accident.

I was under so much stress and in so much fear that I even lost the use of my own body; my injuries wouldn't heal. And the possibility of losing the use of my body was enough to make me think I might lose my mind. And in that moment my greatest fear was realized: I am completely incapable. I can do nothing on my own.

It was my darkest hour, and I purposely did not reach out. I needed to sink or swim alone. I knew I had to do that. And because of doing it alone, I learned my most valuable lesson. I am capable. I can do things on my own. I remembered some words from an old friend of mine, "You just have to keep going." As I continued to fight and struggle, my body began to heal. After that, I battled with the accidents and handled the lawyers, and I did not go bankrupt. Next, I tackled school. I reached inside and got ahold of an inner strength I never knew I had. I got my dissertation together: 125 pages on whiplash. I discovered that whatever I needed to survive had been within me all along. My accident became a powerful aid to introspection, the result of which was earning my degree. Today I know I am capable of doing whatever "it" is because I did it.

Alex was afraid that she didn't have the intelligence or the strength to persevere and complete her dissertation. "I come from a very dysfunctional family, and I grew up with the belief that I was nothing—literally nothing. I was taught that my capabilities lay in my strength of bluffing my way through things. I would never be smart enough to *really* be capable of something. So I think in many ways I was afraid to even try to do something worthwhile. I thought I was an inferior model."

When Alex transcended her fear of feeling inferior, she was able to find the courage to successfully complete her dissertation and earn her doctorate in homeopathy. As Alex told us, "After the accident, when all I could do was lie there, day after day, in pain, trying to research my dissertation, I had to look at my own situation and ask myself: 'What's not allowing me to heal?' Stress, unimaginable lesions around the vertebrae, perpetual agony. When I finally took in the reality of it, I realized that everything I needed to write my dissertation was right inside me. That's what it was all about—homeopathy and my body, my health. And I've adopted that attitude into every aspect of my life. Whatever happens, the power is right here, within me."

◆　　◆　　◆

What can we do when faced with the fear of being inferior? The well-known psychologist, Alfred Adler, coined the term "inferiority complex" and developed a therapy to specifically treat this type of fear. His first step, however, was to give inferiority a new description, as he felt that instead of being a sign of weakness, inferiority was actually a great wellspring of creativity and the motivator by which people could aspire to mastery, success, and completion of their goals. Adler also asserted that what we are born with is not as important as what we do with the abilities we possess. Encouragement is the most distinctive Adlerian procedure, and it is central to all phases of counseling and therapy. He stressed that it is especially important as people consider change in their lives, since encouragement actually means to build courage. Adler felt that courage develops when people become aware of their strengths, when they feel they belong and are not alone, and when they have a sense of hope and can see new possibilities of themselves and their daily living.[8]

LIFTING WEIGHTS LIFTED MY SELF-ESTEEM

Talk about fear, honey. Try standing on a stage in front of five thousand people in China, in a string bikini. Please! But that wasn't the worst of it. I had to dance and I have no rhythm! Oh, it was unbelievable. Can you imagine? Well, to be very honest, I didn't know if I had the guts to do it. I was afraid! Wouldn't you be? But this is how I got there and what happened:

I was standing on a stage with competitors from Hong Kong, Singapore, India, Korea, the Philippines, Indonesia, and China. Blonde, blue-eyed, tanned Canadian me competing in the Eleventh Asian Women's Body-Building Championship in Guangong, China. Categories were light, middle, and heavyweight and were broken down according to age. I was twenty-nine and weighed in at fifty-nine kilos the day of the competition.

Well, the worst of it for me was later, standing all alone on that great big stage for two or three minutes with a selected dance routine and no rhythm wearing a little string bikini. That empty stage was all mine. But what was I going to do? It was either dance or run off the stage! I'm a self-conscious person anyway, about my looks, about my body. My sister was always known as the pretty one. Competing on an international level just kicked in all those insecurities and fears.

So there I am, all alone, little me. Standing on a stage on the other side of the world, staring out at a sea of five thousand Asian heads all staring back at me, floodlights from every direction aimed to highlight every ripple on my body. My heart's pounding. I'm frozen, waiting; you can hear a pin drop, and then I hear my music. And, honey, it just kicked in! I relied on my training! I had hired a choreographer, thank God, and trained with her for months. I had to be there for myself, consistently show up for myself. Day after day I ate and trained exactly the same way. And then the day of the competition—lights, camera, action! I won third in my division! Being the only Caucasian competitor over there, well, it was a big deal. As much as I feared I couldn't do it, I was a winner after all!

Courtney had a fear that if she tried to compete she would lose. "My worst fear is being in a competitive situation and failing," Courtney told us. "Maybe it brings up too many childhood memories of competing with my sister, but I never think I'm of the caliber to compete in anything, really. And in a body-building competition? I had no idea what would happen if I even attempted it. Up there in a bikini? I was terrified!"

When Courtney transcended her fear of competition, she not only placed third in the Eleventh Asian Women's Body-Building Championship, she also saw her business as a personal trainer in Hong Kong increase by over 50 percent. As Courtney said, "I became famous. I had the force of a huge gym behind me, and I became really successful. Being in such a foreign situation and challenging my worst fear like that, it taught me to believe in myself. It taught me I can do anything!"

◆　　◆　　◆

What can we do when faced with a fear of competition? When we're looking for a job, for example, we might experience anxiety when thinking about how many other people are applying for similar positions. Having a few strategies to overcome the fear and anxiety caused by a career move can be invaluable. Here are some tips that we compiled from *The Career Advisor* to help manage the stress of searching for new employment: (1) Acknowledge that you're afraid and itemize your fears. Pretending you aren't afraid can accelerate your fear into terror. (2) Remember some of your past successes in complete detail. (3) Get a mentor. (4) Make a worst-case scenario. What's the worst that could happen? What would you do next? (5) Know yourself and your skills. Know where you are best. (6) Do research. The more you know, the less you will fear a situation. (7) Do relaxation exercises. Meditate. Breathe![9]

MACHISMO

It was early in the morning, and I was sleeping. I don't know how the argument started. I'll never know, but when I woke up, they were shouting at each other—my mother and my brother. It was my brother's birthday. I felt so sad for him. He was twenty-six years old and still living with us, taking care of us—my mother, my five sisters, and me. Ever since my father died, my brother had protected us; that is the way of the Latino culture. The women need looking after. The women must stay in the home and take care of the babies. The women cannot take care of themselves. But I never believed that.

I got out of bed and went to the kitchen. I raised my voice above the shouting, and I told my brother, "You should leave. It's your birthday. You should begin your life." My mother made a kind of raw, scolding sound. I had fought with my mother about this too. I was almost eighteen, and I wanted to go to college. Now we lived in America, and I should be able to have a career. I wanted to be a journalist. But my mother would hear nothing of it. I would get married, and have babies, and be a good wife and mother, just like all my sisters had done.

That is why I was so afraid to leave. There would be no way that I could go to college without disappointing my mother. Without losing my family. No way.

But my brother deserved a life, and I told him! Soon the whole family was arguing. My brother's birthday was ruined. He said to my mother, "Sometimes I wish I could walk out of here and get hit by a car!" I understood what he meant. He was just so tired of all the fighting. So tired. My mother said to him, "If that's what you want, then that's what you should have." I cried when I heard that! She just could not understand the sacrifices my brother and I were making to keep the tradition going for her. It was all for her! She just could not understand! And I said, "How can you say that? He is your son! How can you say such a thing?" I left the house then, with my cousin, and I stayed away until late in the afternoon.

When I came home, my brother, my beautiful brother, he was dead.

He had been hit by a car.

The next day, I left my mother and my sisters, and I did not look back.

RosaMaria was afraid that if she went against her mother's wishes and pursued her dream of becoming a journalist, she would lose her family. RosaMaria told us, "In Latino culture, for a woman to have a career can create many problems, because everyone says: 'You should be married. You should be home taking care of the family.' My sisters, they were all older and married with babies. They were my role models, and my mother. I didn't know what to do. With one foot in my traditional culture and one foot in American culture, I felt like I didn't belong anywhere. When I was sixteen, I tried to commit suicide. I don't think I really wanted to die; I just wanted my family to understand how miserable I was. When my brother died, then they knew."

The tragic death of RosaMaria's brother was the catalyst that allowed her to transcend her fear of disappointing her mother. But RosaMaria Villalpando has found the courage to become a catalyst herself, raising the awareness of many Latina women for whom independence previously seemed impossible. As a TV journalist for the largest Spanish-speaking network in the United States (KMEX), RosaMaria is a Latina success story. As she told us, "I wanted to give the women in my community a voice. They had no options, no information. They needed a voice, and I have tried to do that. I have tried to attend to their needs." Although it took almost a decade, RosaMaria and her mother were finally reunited, and the two now share a deep respect and devotion for each other.

❖   ❖   ❖

What can we do when faced with resistance to our aspirations? In the Latina culture, there is a move toward greater respect, awareness, and understanding. In an article written by author and activist Mira Vidal, it was reported that more and more Latinas are calling for education, employment, and childcare within their community. In the same article, Vidal quoted Francisca Flores, the well-known activist, who perhaps summed it up best with: "Freedom for everyone."[10]

A *FEMALE* SUSHI CHEF?

All the other students and I were standing in line in this Japanese restaurant waiting to have our certificates signed by the master sushi chef. I was the only female. We had just completed the course work and were celebrating our graduation by having lunch together. Our moment of glory had come; it was time for the grand finale. The master was going to sign our certificates of completion. I had scored one hundred on my final exam. One hundred! Still, I was a little apprehensive.

So I'm standing there all excited, moving up in line, inch by inch, and I start to feel a knot of fear roll around in my stomach as I remembered what this man had put me through for so long. He called me stupid and incompetent before he even knew my abilities. I understood he was from another culture, but every single day he had something negative to say about me. As I'm watching the guys in front of me, one by one, bow in reverence and get their certificates signed, I remembered back to my first day of school . . .

I knew there were no female sushi chefs, no one's ever seen one. Still, I was shocked when he commented on my gender. He was dead serious, and seemed truly disgusted that a female was in his class. Every day I got sick from fear and humiliation when he yelled at me and made me the errand girl. It was deeply hurtful. Humiliation *and* offensive slurs? I mean, my God, you can't treat a paying student that way! But I stuck it out and made it through school because what he was doing was so, so wrong. Every day I was actually ill, and I'm no shrinking violet. I had to really find it within myself to rise to the occasion, to literally stand up before him. When he would ask the other students where they wanted to work, he would skip me, and say that I would never get a job. Think about it, have you ever seen a female sushi chef? I felt the sting of tears in my eyes as I stood in line that day watching him signing the other guys' certificates. I thought that the degradation he had inflicted on me was finally over.

So there I was in line, ready to show him; after all I was top of the class in technique and had scored one hundred on my exam! I slid my certificate under his nose. He turned his head, ignoring me. I blanched as I realized the discrimination was, in fact, not over. The memories came flooding back in one big rush when he refused to sign my certificate. I just freaked out on him. I screamed, *"Don't do this! Don't do this! Sign my certificate right now!"* The restaurant was looking at us. He didn't budge. *"Sign this now! Sign it!"* The only way I could finally get him to sign it was to scream and humiliate him in front of everyone.

I got a job at one of the nicest sushi restaurants in town.

Tracy was afraid that if she asked to be treated with respect, the master sushi chef would never sign her certificate of graduation. "I was the only female in the entire class. Right away I knew that my teacher, the master chef, was appalled that I was in the class. He did not want a woman in his class because I would bring dishonor upon his name and reputation. But I really wanted to learn this cuisine. Traditional Japanese cooking is so reverent to the person you're serving—the way you cut the fish, the way you put the plate down—it's all a sign of respect, and I was getting none. It was so difficult, so wrong, and so upsetting!"

When Tracy transcended her fear of demanding respect from the master sushi chef, she obtained her certificate and found the courage to secure employment at a very popular sushi restaurant. In fact, so remarkable was it to see a woman sushi chef that Tracy Griffith was featured by a plethora of media interests. As she told us, "*The L.A. Times* and *Entertainment Tonight*, French and British media coverage, a lot of other overseas news people, and local news people came to interview me. They proudly interviewed me because I was in a totally male-dominated profession. And I feel proud of my work too. People come in all the time and say, 'Wow, I have never seen a female sushi chef!' It's an art that I will always get better at. It gives me a really good feeling, people eating my work, right in front of me. It makes me feel happy and proud."

◆　　◆　　◆

As Tracy's story shows us, sexual discrimination still exists. If you or anyone you know has been sexually harassed or discriminated against in the workplace, call 1-800–669–4000 and ask for the federal Equal Employment Opportunities Commission (EEOC) office nearest you. They will inform you of your rights and the laws pertaining to discrimination in your state.

The Ultimate Success

What is success? Is it defined in terms of money, power, and control? Or as women do we equate success with something more? Something like self-awareness, compassion for others, and personal growth? As we progress into this new century, what do we hope to achieve? For our voice will be heard, louder and louder, as we continue to challenge the status quo and defend ourselves against those who would usurp our freedom.

In her commencement address to Wellesley College in 1997, Oprah Winfrey said, "Create the highest, grandest vision possible for your life because you become what you believe."[11] According to figures compiled by the Merrill Lynch brokerage firm, "Today 27.5

million people, or one out of every four American workers, are employed by women-owned businesses and generate annual sales greater than 3.6 trillion dollars. Women-owned businesses equal 38 percent of all businesses in the U.S. . . . [and] women are branching out into all areas of the economy [including] . . . construction, transportation, communications, agriculture and manufacturing."[12] Women have also taken the greatest mobilizing force this world has ever known and given it a distinctly feminine resonance. It is called the Internet, and more women are involved in this type of communication technology than ever before. Oprah Winfrey with *Oxygen.com*, Ellen Pack of *Woman.com*, and Nancy Evans of *iVillage.com* are just a few of the many women reaching out electronically to share not only the methods of equality, but the means by which to attain it. We can now relay, from the most isolated corners of the earth, the most current information on healthcare, education, employment, childcare, environmental concerns, psychological treatment, and spiritual development.

In 1878, little-known Margaret Wolfe Hungerford coined one of humanity's most profound phrases: "Beauty is in the eye of the beholder."[13] When we look at ourselves, what do we see? More of us have the capacity to reach our full potential than ever before. The beauty we have always held on the inside—our intellect, our intuition, our nurturing wisdom—can finally be seen and *recognized* on the outside. What, then, is success? It is the satisfaction of knowing your worth and the joy of partaking in it. And, ultimately, success must be perceived as the opportunity to just be.

Courage and Health

*How Does Fear Affect
a Woman's Biology?*

Women have been the caretakers of society . . . We are the healer and healed. We are the give and the gift. We are the blessed.

WHAT KIND OF FEAR does health evoke in women? Have you ever felt the sudden, gnawing dread that your health is in jeopardy, and with it the realization that we are mortal after all? The uncertainty of life can fill us with terror at the thought of our own physical limitations, and yet, it is in the knowledge of those limitations that we can become stronger, for with knowledge there is power. The power to heal ourselves, the power to be *good* to ourselves.

But how do we best take care of ourselves?

Although it has long been established that stress is a leading cause of illness for both women and men, it seems that women may have developed a unique means of coping with it. Stress occurs when we are mentally, physically, or emotionally challenged, and our bodies experience an increase in metabolism, an elevation in blood pressure, and a rise in our heart rate and breathing rate. As a recent *Reader's Digest* article outlined, this is called the "fight-or-flight response [and it] works just fine when we do just that—fight or flee. But most often, we do neither. And that's what gets us into trouble. A surplus of unused adrenaline coursing through our bodies can lead to a host of psychological and physical problems."[1] But what if there is a third response to stress? A *woman's* response?

In a recent *Psychology Today Online,* Shelley Taylor, Ph.D., a psychology professor at the University of California, Los Angeles, was reported to have discovered that, for women, the fight-or-flight response is only part of a much bigger picture. Taylor's team has found that, during times of stress, instead of fighting or running away, women are more nurturing and will even assist a person in need. Taylor calls this response to stress: "tend and befriend."[2] In the same article, research by psychologist Tiffany Field, as well as many others, was reported as showing that when we tend and befriend by maintaining a strong support system of family and friends, stress is dramatically reduced, which subsequently results in improved immune function.[3]

Apparently women know that what we give is also what we receive, and it appears to be a key, not only to our emotional happiness, but also to our physical health. In this chapter we will meet women who have overcome disease, injury, infertility, and death to find that by caring for themselves, they've often established stronger, more loving bonds with someone else.

STROKE OF LUCK

It is late December. The law office is quiet and deserted; everyone has either gone home or is away on vacation. Looking down on the dark city street from twenty-six floors above, I can see the forms of holiday shoppers moving along the sidewalks. I am sitting at my desk, holding my pounding head with one hand and a 150-page legal document in the other. Squinting my eyes, I notice the white, twinkle lights on the leafless trees outside begin to blur. Momentary double vision makes my head spin. I try to shake it off, try to blink it away. I'll just work through the rest of this document, and then I'll take a break. Focus. Focus. Concentrate.

My boss left me this case, and I am determined to get it finished. This is an important, sophisticated deal. I've been putting in fourteen-hour days since I started here, so this is not the time to stop. Business isn't that great for the firm right now, but the more extra time I put in, the more I secure my position. A steady career in an unsteady economy. I'm lucky to have this job. But I feel like I'm in a brain fog. The type on the paper looks like it's bleeding into one big mess. Maybe next month I'll take a half-day off. Right now, I just have to focus and concentrate. And just finish this.

Why are the overhead lights getting dim? It's too early for the cleaning crew to be turning them off. It's only 5:30 so it must be my imagination. But this headache; this headache is real, and I have 120 pages to go. I begin to draft the same document for the tenth time. Holding it out, I turn it around and around with my hands, just trying to focus my eyes on what's in front of my face. It's very strange, but I can only see a quarter of the page. The corners are getting dimmer and dimmer, diminishing into a little black dot. Shaking my head a bit, I wonder, is this what they call stars in your eyes? But I must finish this work. I must focus and concentrate.

I see a jagged light. Now a big open space. My headache has become excruciating. In a second I'll take a break. But now I can't see at all because of this blinding pain in my eyes. I'll most definitely lose my job if, in fact, I'm going blind! Extending my hand, I grope for the phone. In complete darkness, I dial 911. I'm thirty-nine years old, and I think I've just had a stroke.

Mary, a high-powered Los Angeles attorney, was afraid that if she said no to her boss, she would lose her job. How many of us have felt a similar pressure at our place of employment? As Mary told us, "Ever since I was eleven years old, I've had this fear of being financially dependent, so I worked. I spent a lot of time baby-sitting when I was a kid, and I put the money away for college. I worked hard to become an attorney, and I was happy to get a job at that firm, but I was always afraid they would replace me with someone else. So, again, I worked very hard to stay. I became the buffer between two men—the man managing the law firm and my boss who didn't want to work. So I ended up doing all the work."

When Mary transcended her fear of losing her job, she became healthier than she'd ever been before which, in turn, allowed her to rediscover her family. She also found the courage to begin a new career. Mary told us, "I had a total of five strokes. Before the strokes, my marriage was in trouble, and I rarely saw my kids. After the strokes, I had to accept that I couldn't work as hard as I once did, but that gave me the time to spend with my children, and my relationship with my husband is back on track. In fact, we even had another baby. I also became my own boss, so I can set my own hours, and

I've finally realized that I can do whatever I need to do, *even if that is nothing.* I now know how to say no."

◆　　◆　　◆

What can we do when faced with the fear of a career setback or job loss, which then results in unhealthful stress? An article for the website *www.onhealth.com* recently reported: "'The way in which a woman responds to daily stress can affect her risk of having a stroke,' say University of Pittsburgh researchers." The same article continues, "[The University off Pittsburgh] study shows that women whose heart rates and blood pressure rise during mental stress have a greater risk of developing accelerated arteriosclerosis, a disease in which blood vessels become clogged with fat deposits and block blood from reaching the heart or brain."[4]

However, researcher Karen Sutton-Tyrell told *onhealth*: "Being aware of your reactivity [to stress] is the first step [to good health]." She also reported that exercise could be the most important way for women to better manage and alleviate stress in their lives.[5]

FOOD FOR COMFORT AND DEFENSE

I struggle to lift myself out of bed, reaching for my crutches. With one broken ankle, I hobble to the bathroom, already sick and tired of the effort it takes just to turn on the shower. I've been out of bed thirty seconds, and I feel something deep inside me threaten to explode. As I remove my nightclothes, I am careful not to catch a glimpse of my reflection in the mirror. Steadying myself, I carefully step into the shower, moving my hands from the support of the crutches to the support of the soap dish. This is awful! As I try to prop myself up and turn the water on, I almost lose my balance and just manage to avoid another fall. But it shakes me up; it rattles my nerves. The last time I took a fall it caused me to break this ankle in three places. I feel the tears sting at my eyes. As the water from the shower pours down on me, something inside releases, and I cry and I cry and I cry.

I've always been overweight. This armor that has protected me has also kept me a bystander of life. Food has always been a comfort, but it's also been a defense! I've allowed it to protect me from life, and now it's hurting me. Realizing this causes me to become nearly hysterical in my torrent of tears. I cry my defenses away: "I never thought I would become so reliant on others at this young age. I can't make my bed while on crutches. I can't drive. I wish I could date; I wish I could change. But I'm afraid, I'm afraid, I'm afraid!"

As my defenses wash down the drain, I understand for the first time that in order to take care of my body, I have to take care of my head. With this awareness, I feel clean and clear. My tears have begun to subside. Turning off the water, I reach for the crutches, then a towel. Slowly drying my body and my eyes, I finally look up into the mirror. There's something different there. Something that is ready to become fully alive.

Gretchen was afraid that if she lost her physical weight, she'd be emotionally defenseless. As Gretchen told us, "I was 256 pounds when I took a small fall on a staircase and broke my ankle. I had to have surgery. There are eight screws and a plate holding my fibula together, and two long screws inside my foot. But until the accident, I thought my weight was my best defense. I really wore it like armor. It protected me from everything I was afraid of—dating, falling in love, getting hurt. The weight makes you feel safe, but you're not."

When Gretchen transcended her fear of becoming emotionally defenseless if she lost weight, she found the courage to truly begin to live. She told us, "My accident was the catalyst, and because I made it through, I began to trust my inner strength. That's what really matters, trusting in yourself, then you know you can handle whatever happens. I'm really engaged in life now. Being emotionally hurt or happy, I know I can handle it." With the advice of a medical doctor and the counsel of a therapist, Gretchen Gray continues to lose weight and has begun to do things she never thought she would be able to do, like hiking, skydiving, and wearing a bathing suit to the beach.

◆　　◆　　◆

What can we do if the fear of emotional stress causes us to gain unhealthy weight? As reported for *Reuters Health,* Dr. Elissa Epel, at the University of California at San Francisco has discovered that there is a link between stress and unhealthy weight gain. Dr. Epel says, "Psychological stress may increase abdominal fat in healthy people."[6] The same study also found that women with high levels of abdominal fat, regardless of whether the rest of their bodies were fat or thin, were more vulnerable to stress.[7]

In a report by Richard B. Parr, Ed.D., for *Physician and Sportsmedicine,* overwhelming research shows that the benefits of exercise can reach far beyond fitness and weight control. As he tells us, "Physical activity lowers your risk of heart disease, stroke, high blood pressure, and diabetes. In addition, overweight people can boost their self-control, self-confidence, and well-being, as well as lessen stress and depression."[8]

Always consult with a medical doctor before starting a new exercise program.

A DIABETIC OVERCOMES HER FEAR OF NEEDLES

You just never know who your angels are or when they're going to appear or disappear.

I've had diabetes since I was four years old. Later in my life, my best friend, Kathryn, took care of me because I wouldn't take care of myself. She was an angel in mortal's clothes. I remember countless episodes at the hospital when I would awaken from unconsciousness to look up into Kathryn's face. I've had thousands of insulin attacks and with all the complications, the body just begins to break down. To make matters worse, I wouldn't give myself my shots. I denied my disease as much as I could. Doctor after doctor gave me death sentence after death sentence. "You could lose your kidneys, your heart, possibly the use of your legs." But I would just brush it off. Kathryn, though, would try to convince me, "Holly, it's okay to take care of yourself." She was everything to me. Then, just like that, one day Kathryn was snatched right out of the sky. My angel just vanished from sight. After Kathryn died in a plane crash, I ignored my diabetes completely. I slept twenty-two hours a day.

Six months later, someone convinced me to go to a party. I met another angel that night, a man. I don't know how else to describe it, but we had such a deep connection. When we looked into each other's eyes it was familiar, as if we'd known each other a long time. Anyway, we dated for two years and then one night, we had been driving around in his car, and we stopped. It was late and quiet, and he told me that he loved me. He said he cared about me so much, that for the first time in his life, he was thinking about marriage and family. There was something about him that made me feel alive in a way I had never felt before. We did a pinky swear and promised we would never leave each other. Later that year, we were married.

That night in the car something was stirring in the sky, my angel was there, because that was the moment I really understood about self-care. That was the spark that ignited the fire: I had someone else to consider besides myself.

Holly was afraid that if she took care of and loved herself, she would lose the love of those she needed most. As Holly told us, "My parents denied my diabetes, and I felt like it was not okay to have it. They couldn't acknowledge the disease; therefore, it was not okay to take care of myself. But I was always very afraid of how I was feeling, health wise. Kathryn was the only person who really took care of me, and when she died, I had a hard time going on."

When Holly transcended her fear of self-care, she realized that those who truly loved her would love her regardless of her diabetes, and that gave her the courage to love herself. "Meeting my husband literally changed my life," Holly told us. "I began to take care of myself, for me and for him. I learned how to give myself my own shot by thinking of it as a friend. The needle was giving me life, and life felt good. Taking care of myself was finally okay."

◆　　◆　　◆

How can we transcend the fear of taking care of ourselves? In Holly's case, not only was she anxious about caring for her diabetes, she was also suffering from the tragic death of her best friend. In a recent article for *Medconsult.com*, it was reported that "[There is] growing evidence that depression and anxiety may play a role in diabetes [as] researchers from the Medical College of Ohio have found that biofeedback and relaxation therapy can reduce blood sugar levels in people who are not suffering from depression or anxiety disorder."[9] When we care for ourselves and treat ourselves to something like simple relaxation, even our blood sugar levels are reduced.

It is important to remember that diabetes can be a dangerous disease that requires the immediate care of a physician.

WHEN I LET GO OF CONTROL, THE LIFE INSIDE ME BEGAN TO GROW

The phone rang; it was my doctor. I sensed the urgency even before he spoke. I would have to make a decision. A life or death decision. But what if I made the wrong one? I asked my husband. I asked my mom. I asked my dad. They tried to find me an answer, but time was running out. I was in a panic, crying and crying, and then something, I don't know what, just came over me. I turned to my mom and said, "I want to see a rabbi."

I am not a very spiritual person, yet I went to the synagogue in search of a man I didn't know. Finally I found him and explained the severity of my situation. He told me to slow down and stay calm, that it would be all right. But he didn't understand how hard it had been! I tried to explain about the fertility shots and the pain that comes with them, and the months and months of trying, and waiting, and worrying, and failing. So many times we had tried to get pregnant, and each time we had failed. I did not think I could live with another failure. But I might not live if we went on with the procedure. My ovaries had been overstimulated. I could die if we didn't stop.

Oh, but I wanted a baby so much!

The rabbi listened, and nodded, and told me what everyone else had told me: it was my decision. But I didn't know what to do! Out of desperation, I asked a question I had never asked before: "What is the weekly chapter in the Torah?" The Torah is the Jewish bible, written in the ancient text, which I can barely understand. But for some reason I asked to see it, and he opened the book, and I managed to decipher some of the lines.

It was the story of Abraham and his wife, Sarah. I read on. God had promised Abraham and Sarah a child, but as time passed and Sarah didn't become pregnant, she was considered barren, and all hopes for a baby had been put aside. Then one day, when Sarah was ninety years old, God came disguised as a person and told her that soon she would be pregnant. Sarah and her friends had laughed and laughed at this because they thought it was so preposterous—a ninety-year-old woman becoming pregnant! But nine months later, miraculously, Sarah gave birth to Isaac.

My fear was gone. I had had a sign. I closed the Torah and sat there for a moment, calm as could be. I had done everything I could do. Now it was time to give up control. Let whatever was going to happen, happen. I would delay the procedure; it was the best I could do. And with that decision, I felt great peace.

The next day we went to the clinic, and I was out of danger. The overstimulation was gone. The doctor was amazed! But I knew it was the calm.

Nine months later, miraculously, I gave birth to our son.

Hilla was afraid, in this matter of life and death, to make a detrimental decision. As Hilla told us, "I didn't know what to do. To save my life? To risk my life to have a child? I kept thinking of all the fertility shots, all the pain, all the emotional stress, all the physical stress—that it would all be for nothing. I was too afraid to make any kind of decision at all."

When Hilla transcended her fear of making a life or death decision, she was not only able to make a choice, she made a very beneficial one. Hilla's baby was born nine months later, a healthy, happy boy. "When I read the passage about Abraham's wife, Sarah, having a baby at ninety years old, and laughing and laughing because it was so outrageous, I guess I surrendered. Because, with today's technology, it *is* possible for a woman, who would have been considered barren even twenty years ago, to have a child. And I began to trust."

◆　　◆　　◆

The birth of a child has always been considered a miracle, and now, as assisted reproductive technology (ART) continues to advance, infertile couples have a very good chance of having children. According to a booklet put out by Serono Laboratories, thousands of women become pregnant each year using ART, and those results get better as time goes on.[10] Besides the latest in ART advancements, there are also a variety of support groups and counseling available through organizations such as RESOLVE and the American Society for Reproductive Medicine (ASRM). As Hilla told us, "It takes courage to try something new, but when you are infertile, courage is exactly what will bring new life to you."

FEELING YOUNG AGAIN

I stood on the block trying to find the courage to hoist my leg over his back, and my hip was hurting.

The horse was big, 16.2 hands, and he was so beautiful. I ran my trembling hand over his sleek, bay coat and caressed his dark brown mane. I was really nervous. Did he sense it? Maybe he was wondering the same thing I was. What was I doing at fifty-seven years old taking up riding again? I'd quit riding fifteen years ago, very soon after I'd taken a terrible fall. At that time, my horse had bolted out of control, and I'd landed smack into a tree. I'd cracked a couple of my ribs, blackened my eye, but the worst of it was, as I'd slid down the bark, my shirt had come up, and I'd literally torn the skin right off my back! How could I possibly want to ride again?!

I looked down at my husband and my daughter, who were both smiling up at me, waiting for me to get on the horse. For years I've been watching my daughter—she and her horse looked so perfect jumping over the white fences—and I secretly longed to be in her place, but I knew I'd never do it. Even though I love horses, I knew I'd never have the courage. But my husband must have seen my hidden desire, and he bought a horse. This horse.

I took a deep breath. It was a gorgeous spring day. Not a cloud in the sky. The green fields lay before me, and the pretty outdoor riding ring was beckoning. It was all so very beautiful. The horse nuzzled my thigh, as if to say, "Get on! We'll be wonderful together!"

I was terrified, my hip hurt, in fact my whole body started to hurt as if in anticipation of another fall, but I got on, and suddenly I felt like a youngster. No more aches and pains. It was the most exhilarating feeling!

I felt free.

Jean was afraid that she would suffer a serious injury, as well as more aches and pains, if she began riding again. As we get older, especially if we've had an injury, we may become afraid of participating in physical activities, no matter what they are. As Jean told us, "My fear of that past accident was dictating my future. I really wanted to try again, but I was so nervous! So I refused something for fifteen years, something I *loved* to do."

In transcending her fear of riding a horse again, Jean not only found the courage to return to her passion of riding horses, but she has also found a way to get rid of her aches and pains. Jean told us, "I've been riding again for twelve years, and I've never felt better. The excitement of the sport makes all my aches and pains go away. I had wanted to prove to my family that I could do it, but what I found was that getting back up on a horse was one of the best things I've ever done for myself."

❖　　❖　　❖

What can we do when faced with losing our passions to the fear of injury or aging? Chiropractor Philip T. Santiago calls physical exercise the "ultimate anti-aging pill." In an article for *chiroweb.com*, Dr. Santiago goes on to say, "One of [my] first recommendations is exercise. Many people assume that getting fatter, weaker and stiffer is inevitable with age. A growing body of research, however, suggests that much of the decline attributed to aging actually comes from being sedentary.

People who are physically fit, eat a healthy, balanced diet and take nutritional supplements can measure out to be ten to twenty years younger biologically than their chronological age."[11]

THE SUPREME DONATION

Nurses. Nurses in green scrubs surround me. Looking into their eyes, I wonder, how can we ever really know how someone else is feeling? Flat on my back, I stare beyond their faces—up to the rows and rows of squares that line the hospital ceiling. Maybe if I count them it will prevent me from thinking. Thinking. This is the right thing to do. I know that this is the right thing. No question, because he would do the same for me. But what will our lives be like after today? Will I survive this? Will he? God, are you there? Are you listening?

"It will be just a few more minutes now, Tess. The doctor is on his way."

They've rolled me into a different room, another reality. Squinting up into chrome-covered light bulbs, I turn my head away. It's so stark in here. I feel so alone. I feel so afraid. I wonder, will anyone want me after this? Will I ever be attractive again? Are thoughts like this selfish considering the grand scheme of things? What differences will I encounter in my life that I haven't even thought of today? The only thing that I'm sure of is that I have to do this. These fears are normal, the decision is made; I must be brave.

"The doctor is here now, Tess. You'll just feel a little pinch, and then you'll start to fall asleep."

A little pinch and here I go. Pray for me mother and dad. But what other choice did I have? It's all been planned. It's all been arranged. If I never awaken, my daughter is in good hands, but how do you replace a mother? You can't. Nor can you replace a brother. I feel myself slipping away . . . It's okay; it's okay . . . I'm doing everything I can. My brother . . . my brother is dying . . . but there is life in my body that can help save his. My last conscious thought before I drift away is, with God's help . . . and my kidney . . . we both will live.

Tess was afraid that the quality of her life would be compromised, if not lost, if she donated a kidney to her brother. As Tess told us, "I was afraid that my health wouldn't be as good. I was afraid of the scar, and what man would ever want a woman with this huge scar? I had a fear of not waking up after the surgery. I had a fear about dying. I had a fear that my daughter would be left without a mother. I had emotional fears and physical fears and external fears."

When Tess transcended her fear of donating her kidney to her brother, she found the courage to start a new life. "Before the surgery, I was having a very rough time. I had recently divorced. I was at a crossroads in my career. I'd even considered suicide. But my brother was going to die. That was the bottom line. This was someone I cared about and loved so I stepped up to the plate. After the surgery, I became involved with the hospital where the surgery was performed and began a support group. I started giving training to both donors and receivers. I was told I had a gift and that I should go back to school to become a therapist." Tess Hightower is now a successful psychotherapist in Beverly Hills; she raises money and recruits celebrities to help promote organ donation.

❖   ❖   ❖

How can we face the fear of losing something of ourselves, possibly even our own life, to help someone else? The act of giving can have a profound affect not only on our state of mind, but also on our health. For instance, a study reported by *Daniel Freeman Hospitals* concluded that "Volunteers feel healthier than nonvolunteers . . . and volunteering helps reduce stress while boosting happiness and self-esteem. Volunteers may even live longer. A study of 17,000 Swedes revealed that for every 3.7 socially 'isolated' people who died, only one socially 'involved' person died."[12]

A recent article from *Fitness* reported an American Medical Association study which found that people with more social involvement have a greater resistance to upper respiratory illness than those who are less social. In the same article, Sheldon Cohen, Ph.D., professor of psychology at Carnegie-Mellon University, explained: "Social support helps reduce stress, which suppresses the immune system."[13]

REFUSING TO BELIEVE

I discovered that I was sick as a result of a car accident I had been in ten years ago. I went in for a CT scan to see why my injuries weren't healing. The first doctor who saw me said he thought I had lupus and that I'd probably had it for eight years. I didn't believe him. It was just that simple.

So I went to doctor number two, and he said the same—that I had lupus. Doctors number three, four, and five all gave me the same diagnosis, but I refused to believe. Then number seven, a big-time Beverly Hills specialist, told me that doctors one through six were wrong. Doctor seven said I had fibromyalgia. And *that* I believed—because it was a far less severe disease. The strange thing was, my symptoms didn't match the diagnosis for fibromyalgia. But doctor number seven said I was too young to have lupus, and I agreed.

I continued to get sicker. Despite the medications, the treatment plans, the emotional and physical therapy, I was becoming gravely ill. I became so sick and inflamed that one day my throat began to swell shut. I was suffocating to death. Every movement I made was agonizing, and I finally had to admit to myself that I must have lupus. In the ambulance, I kept hearing the words I'd been told over and over again: "With a diagnosis of lupus, you have only five to ten years to live . . . five to ten years to live."

After the emergency room doctor revived me back to consciousness, she said, "Eight more hours and you would have been dead."

Shaun was afraid that if she accepted her diagnosis of lupus, she would die. Shaun told us, "I was able to accept the fibromyalgia because it's a far more benign type of illness. But lupus is an autoimmune disease, meaning it can cause the body to harm its own healthy cells and tissues, and that can lead to inflammation of the lungs, heart, kidneys, brain, and joints. I was so afraid of lupus, I had to deny the possibility of its existence. I just couldn't handle the thought of it. It seemed like a death sentence."

When Shaun transcended the fear of accepting her illness, she found the courage to do the most important thing of all—she began to treat it. "I was locked into being a victim," Shaun told us. "I wasn't taking care of myself, and I had to change my life in order to live. I did a lot of research, took loads of herbs and vitamins, changed my diet, and started receiving acupuncture. I don't spend my time being negative. I went back to school for my master's degree. And I pray a lot. I pray for other people. Not only does it make me feel good to care for someone else, but I look forward to seeing them get better." Shaun seems to be getting better all the time. Diagnosed with lupus ten years ago, in the past year she has received a clean bill of health. As she told us, "It's like a miracle. There is no sign of it in my blood tests. Absolutely none."

◆　　◆　　◆

What can we do when confronted with the fear of a life-threatening illness? The first thing to do, of course, is to receive and maintain specific medical care and follow your doctor's orders.

There have been several recent studies concerning health and the healing power of prayer. As reported in *Newsweek*, Dr. Dale Matthews and the Arthritis Treatment Center in Clearwater, Florida, have found evidence to support, at the very least, a short-term health benefit to prayer.[14] And in a recent *Newsweek* poll, it was determined that 79 percent of Americans believe that God answers prayers for healing someone with an incurable disease.[15]

FEELINGS WERE NOT ENCOURAGED

What am I doing here? I'm nothing like you people. The Betty Ford Center, another group meeting, and it's always the same thing. You all sit around and talk about your "feelings." Please. It seems so self-centered.

That woman over there? I will never, ever expose myself on a group level the way that she just did. Talk about those personal things like that? Not me. Oh, no, not the men too! I can't believe that man over there is going to . . . he's standing up, introducing himself, and . . . oh, my God, his voice is shaking. Surely, he's not going to cry?! If he does, I'm going to get up and walk out of this room. Another man is talking about *his* feelings. Now everyone is laughing. Laughing and crying. I don't know which is worse, laughing or crying. I mean, how could anyone find anything to laugh about in a situation like this? Well, it might be the way they do things in "twelve-step," but not me. Emotions and communication, no thank you. I don't need either one because I'm stronger than these people.

"Hi, I'm Maggie. I'm an addict. I know a lot of people in this room have had a hard time with their parents, but I really, really love mine. I love my dad more than anyone else on earth. He's so strong and honorable. More than anything else, I just wanted him to love me, and I always thought the way to do that was to be like him."

Now that I can relate to: a girl, my age, who actually loves her dad. Dad. He must be so ashamed of me. I really let him down, and all I ever wanted to do was to make him proud. I refuse to start crying in front of these strangers. But every one of my accomplishments, everything I did, I did for him. Still, right now it all feels so false. I feel like I failed him. And I know it's because of the drugs. Drugs, right now they sound pretty good.

"My father is from a different generation and a different culture. For him, not feeling his feelings was part of his survival skills, but he's not me. Feelings are a natural part of living. But because I wasn't comfortable with mine, I numbed them with drugs and alcohol."

Listening to that girl talk about her experience makes me feel like I've been kicked in the stomach. I feel like the wind has been knocked out of me. I feel the sting of tears in my eyes. Is that it? Is that why I have been using drugs? Because I'm uncomfortable with emotions?

Something inside me just clicked; it's like a light has just turned on in my head. Tingles rush up and down my spine. Communication. Emotions. We don't show affection or sadness in my family; we never cry. All this time I've been afraid of my own feelings—*that's* why I've been numbing them with drugs.

Christina was afraid of feeling her own feelings because she thought they might hurt her. How many of us have suppressed our feelings in the fear that they might be too painful? As Christina told us, "We never discussed our problems in my family, but when we moved to America from the Philippines, everything was so different. We needed to talk about it! I was only ten, but I remember being very depressed about the move. Still, all I got from my father was that he wanted me to be perfect. We were in America now. My grades had to be perfect, I had to be perfect; it was very hard. I started becoming afraid to fail, to fail my father. Fail in front of my friends. That's when I started using cocaine. It gave me the energy to excel in school and gain the acceptance of my peers. But most of all, it numbed my fear. Numbed my emotions. I was just so afraid that if I failed no one would love me anymore."

When Christina transcended her fear of feeling her emotions, she began to heal her relationships, particularly with her father. Christina told us, "Being in a twelve-step program really clarified a lot for me. I realized I was afraid of my own feelings. I was living for everyone else, and not myself. Now I know what's important to me, and how to get it. I express my feelings too. In fact, I found out I'm a very expressive, creative person. I like photography and poetry, and I'm developing my own web site. And, finally, my father and I can say to each other, 'I love you.'"

A *Chicago Tribune* article reported that "Just as certain genes make some people more prone to heart disease, cancer or Alzheimer's disease, scientists now believe other genes may make them more susceptible to becoming addicted . . ."[16] The same article found that between sixty and seventy million Americans had tried an illegal drug sometime in their lives, and 4.2 million had become addicted. Also, sixty-five million Americans were reported to drink alcohol, with slightly more than eight million becoming addicted.[17] In Wayne Kritsberg's book, *The Adult Children of Alcoholics Syndrome*, he suggests that addiction, for some people, can act as a substitute for the feelings of a healthy relationship that they never had as young children.[18]

It takes courage to become sober, but as Christina told us, "It is the best thing I ever did in my life."

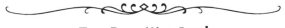

THIS BABY WILL LIVE!

I am sitting in my kitchen, my head in my hands. My baby girl, Tessa, is dying. She is only four years old, and she has been diagnosed with incurable brain cancer. I have AVM—arteriovenous malformation. It's a malformed artery in my brain. It hurts so much right now. It could kill me. Maybe I will die with my daughter. We have brought her home from the hospital to die; I would like to die. Maybe if I feel enough stress, enough hurt, enough hell, God will finally take me, burst that artery, something. Please, God, take me, or tell me why you let me live to deliver my Tessa? At twenty-five years old, I was five months pregnant, and I had a stroke. That's when the doctors discovered the AVM. They told me I was a walking time bomb. A walking pregnant time bomb.

I look up at the sliver of moon outside the kitchen window; it barely casts a light. Suddenly, my head feels like it is in a vice, being crushed. Tighter, tighter.

How could you do this, God? Now our adopted baby boy is dying too! We had wanted Tessa to have a little brother and had gone through the process of adopting a baby from Colombia, but now my husband tells me that our little boy was born prematurely and won't make it through the night. Why, God?! What purpose could this pain and suffering serve?

Tessa does not have a chance, but maybe . . . ?

I don't quite realize I'm on the phone to Colombia, to the doctor there. I don't quite realize what I am saying through all these thousands of miles. "None of us knows whether we're going to make it through the night!" I am shouting. "But this baby will live! *This boy will live!*"

I try to convince the doctor to work harder. I try to convince myself to survive.

In the morning, the boy is still alive.

So am I.

Marianne was afraid that, with the suffering she was forced to endure with her own serious health condition, the death of her daughter would kill her one way or another. As Marianne told us, "I had always feared the pain, literally feared the pain that the AVM caused me. I had cluster migraine headaches, sometimes as many as ten, even fifteen a day. When they told me Tessa was going to die, the pain became even worse. It was like living in hell—in a torture chamber. And then, when they told me that the infant boy we were going to adopt was also going to die, I thought of suicide."

When Marianne took up the cause of her adopted son, she transcended the fear of losing her daughter and of losing her own life. "When I found the courage to turn my focus toward someone else, someone I could possibly help, it helped me. I survived—which a lot of doctors didn't expect. I've even had the AVM surgically removed, and the doctors didn't think I would survive that either. The doctor who removed it called it a miracle, but I think miracles happen all the time, when we reach out."

Marianne Merz and her husband have gone on to adopt two more children from Colombia, and Marianne also gives a great deal of time to her friends. One friend in particular is Susan, who we will meet in the next story.

◆　　◆　　◆

What can we do when faced with the fear of losing our own life or that of a loved one? The benefit of having someone else to focus on, other than ourselves, seems to be a key factor to our good health. A recent *Newsweek* reported that psychologist Thomas Karmarck, in a University of Pittsburgh study, asked thirty-nine college-age women to count down from the thousands by seventeens, and to do it fast. They were instructed to count once alone, and once accompanied by a friend. Not surprisingly, both tests showed stress on the women's cardiovascular systems, but more importantly, having a friend there reduced the impact by half.[19]

SUPPORTIVE SOUL SISTERS

I was very afraid when I was diagnosed with breast cancer, but when you've got a friend who you can talk to, who knows what you're going through, a lot of that fear goes away. Marianne helped my fear go away.

I was getting weaker and weaker. I didn't know why. The doctors thought it was my gall bladder. With the sonogram they found out I had liver cancer, and then they gave me a mammogram. I'd been getting annual mammograms for a long time, so I didn't think anything could be wrong with my breasts. But they found cancer, and it was the primary cancer. In other words, the breast cancer was there first, and it metastasized or spread to my liver. I have Stage 4 breast cancer. But before I could have a mastectomy, they had to treat the liver cancer right away, along with the breasts, so for almost five months I had chemotherapy. Then I had a bilateral mastectomy. I was really afraid.

When Marianne and I met, we realized we had a lot of health issues in common, a lot of suffering. But we'd talk on the phone, and we'd try to make each other laugh. We'd laugh and laugh, and really cheer each other up. I call her my little soul sister. We're only two years apart, and we understand each other so well. Sometimes, when the chemo would have me really worn out, Marianne would bring my husband and me dinner. She'd bring everything. The lasagna, the salad, the salad dressing, the garlic bread, the wine, everything! We'd talk, and laugh. And little by little, with a friend like Marianne, I wasn't afraid anymore.

I'm just not afraid.

Because she has both Stage 4 breast cancer and liver cancer, Susan was afraid she would die, very quickly, without having the time to really stop and appreciate her life. As Susan told us, "I used to be a clothing buyer. I was in a rat race, traveling all the time. Days would go by, and I wouldn't even know it. I used to let my career run me, and I really took the rest of my life—my love for my husband, my love for animals, and nature—for granted."

When Susan transcended her fear of dying without first appreciating life, she not only found the courage to truly appreciate her life, but she also began to feel better. As Susan Fuller told us, "I was always so stressed. I'd even scrutinize my bank statements to the last penny. But now I try to enjoy my life. I know what experiences are really important, and which ones aren't. Ironic as it sounds, I think I have what everyone dreams of—my husband and good friends like Marianne. I really have everything. I have love." Both Susan's breast cancer and her liver cancer are, remarkably, in remission.

◆　　◆　　◆

How can we transcend the fears that keep us from fully appreciating our lives? It seems that love truly is life. In a *Newsweek* study, heart patients were asked whether they felt loved. Those who felt the least loved had 50 percent more arterial damage than those who felt most loved.[20] *Newsweek* also reported on a study run by Dr. David Spiegel of Stanford in which eighty-six advanced breast cancer patients were followed, fifty of whom joined small support groups as part of their treatment. Four years later, a third of those receiving the extra support were still alive. Every one of the control patients (those patients who didn't join a support group) had died.[21]

When You've Got Your Health

When you've got your health, you've got everything. It's something our mothers probably repeated to us, over and over, until we got tired of hearing it. And yet when we are sick, it is most likely our first thought. When we feel sick, we long to be well, and we tell ourselves that from that point on we'll take better care of ourselves. We'll treat ourselves right.

But do we?

A recent *Reader's Digest* report said that according to the American Institute of Stress in Yonkers, New York, as many as 90 percent of visits to primary care physicians are stress related.[22] We now know that stress can be greatly responsible for the suppression of our immune systems, and that in order to remain in good health, we must find a way to manage our stress. A *Newsweek* report on stress explained that in times of crisis, the stress hormones—adrenaline, noradrenaline, and cortisol—switch the entire body into an emergency mode.[23] And as Stanford biologist Robert Sapolsky told *Newsweek*, "[If] every day is an emergency you pay a price [to your health]."[24] In essence, we must find a way to manage our fear, for fear is what causes the stress hormones to surge through our bodies, and when they go unused, it can cause illness. As women, how can we manage, and even alleviate, the stress in our lives?

In an article for *Psychology Today Online*, Dr. Shelly E. Taylor, Ph.D., who has discovered that women have a third response to stress, says, "Fight or flight is basically a response that doesn't involve the hands-on protection of others. But [in a long-ago world] females needed to protect their young, and affiliating with a social group [rather than fighting or fleeing] afforded more protection for females . . . which could be the basis for why women under stress today are inclined to 'tend and befriend.'"[25] In the same article, Dr. Taylor and her colleagues reported to have found that oxytocin, a hormone that has been linked to maternal behavior and social affiliation appears to play a major role in the response of many women to stress, as those individuals with high oxytocin levels are calmer, more social, and less anxious.[26] When women lend a helping hand we assist, even on a hormonal level, in maintaining our own health, too.

Women have been the caretakers of society. We have nursed both the young and old and have offered a shoulder to cry on in times of turmoil. We are the arms that embrace when all else fails. We are the warmth in the spirit and the kindness in the heart. We are the all-forgiving mother. We are the true and loyal friend. We are the love in times of conflict and the inspiration in times of peace. We are all of these things. And now we know that this very ability to extend a helping hand, in turn, will extend our own lives. We are the healer and the healed. We are the giver and the gift. We are the blessed.

Courage and Danger

What Do Women Fear Most?

As women of courage, we will

prevail upon society to

transcend the antiquated days of

shadow and myth.

WHAT KIND OF FEAR does danger evoke in women? Do we run from a threat, or do we attack it? Do we freeze like a wide-eyed animal caught in a trap?

It used to be that most of us would have answered the latter, because for centuries women felt trapped, not by jagged fetters, but by the dark, ominous presence of danger. Even as little girls, our fairy tales warned of what might befall us if we were to take an unattended step outside the proverbial castle walls. We were introduced to tale after tale of woe and dread, for to be a woman was to be a fragile maiden, lovely to look at, yet hardly a match for the many dragons that roamed the countryside. So we remained fearful inside the castle, and when we did venture out, we had no means of protecting ourselves but to call upon the valiant knight.

But how do we respond to danger now?

The answer for many of us is that as we become more independent and empowered, we are refusing to accept danger in our lives anymore. We don't want it on our streets, in our homes, at our place of work, in our personal relationships. We're sickened by the escalation of violence that so many of us have to face, sometimes on a daily basis. We feel abused, exploited, betrayed—and we're ready to fight back.

During the past decade, more women have fought the dragon—the violent acts that have been perpetrated against us—than ever before. We have devised powerful legislation like the Violence Against Women Act, a landmark bill passed by Congress in 1994 that stipulates a complete eradication of violence against women in the United States. We have ever-more strident stalking laws, sexual assault laws, sexual harassment laws, and the cooperation of nearly every single government agency in our quest for justice. We can choose from a wide array of organizations that provide education on how to defend ourselves against both physical and psychological abuse, and we can take advantage of nonprofit women's shelters, legal assistance centers, and workplace violence seminars.

In a recent PBS documentary film about violence against women, a forty-nine-year-old Salt Lake City woman relayed her story of rape, saying, "I know I will never, ever be the same person again. In fact, after it happened, I asked both my daughter and my sister if I looked different. Because I felt like I was so changed."[1]

Women's lives can, and have been, changed by acts of violence and degradation. But we are no longer bound by the castle walls; we have emerged from behind them. We have learned wisdom and determination from brutality and domination. We are not obliged to wait for the valiant knight on his swift white charger to come to our rescue.

The following women will show just how far we've traveled from that era, for in finding the strength to slay the dragon, they also exposed the fairy tale for what it *truly* is: the fear that, ultimately, we cannot defend or fight for ourselves. However, as each woman and her story prove, not only can we protect ourselves, we do protect ourselves.

OBSESSION

My handbag was still on my arm and my keys in my hand. *"What are you plotting now, bitch? To leave me? You're too stupid to make it on your own!"*

I had just returned home after a pleasant Sunday lunch. My heart raced as Richard, my husband, approached. I could feel a thin veil of perspiration spring up on the palms of my hands as I recognized the dark storm twisting in his eyes. I inched away from him. He turned and violently kicked the wall. Then with a raised fist, he slammed a hole into the door. Looking around the kitchen, his jealous frenzy was escalating quickly. He hurled a five-gallon water jug against the wall, and I thought to myself, "He's not going to hit the wall anymore. I'm going to be next, and he's probably going to kill me!"

Glancing to the side, my heart racing, I knew I had to somehow get past him, down the stairs, and out of the house. All I could think was, "Maybe while he is smacking the wall I can get away!" And I did. I managed to run down the stairs to the front lawn, where I was yelling at the top of my voice, "Don't hurt me, Richard! Please, please, don't hurt me!" Praying that someone would call the police, I remember seeing a neighbor lift and peek through their blinds, then lower them. I had seen this side of my husband all too often; the demon inside him was ruthless. But no one came to help.

Now on the grass with my car in sight, Richard took several long strides toward me and shoved me. He pulled at my purse, trying to claim my only means to freedom—the keys to my car. When he was looking around to see whether anyone was watching, I edged backward and reached my vehicle. My entire body was shaking, but I managed to get the key into the lock. After slamming the car door closed and the lock down, to my horror I saw Richard reach into his pocket and bring out a second set of keys!

His face was contorted with insanity, upper lip curled back like a rabid dog. He peered down at me through the window and growled obscenities. He unlocked the lock. Hysterical, I slammed it back down with my left hand, while with my right I tried to start the engine. He repeatedly unlocked the door, and I kept pounding it down until I was crying and the palm of my hand was bruised. In my terror, time stood still. In what could have been my last moments on earth, I managed to get the car in reverse and drive away with my life.

Barb was afraid that if she tried to leave her husband, he would kill her. "I was terrified of him. His anger was so quick, and his rages were awful. He was suspicious of everything I did, and he would call the places I worked, spying on me. I found out that he was even recording my telephone conversations. But I was just too terrified of his temper to walk out." This fear is not unusual. Many women stay in abusive relationships for this exact reason, often too intimidated to report their partner's repeated violent behavior to friends, much less authorities. As Barb told us, "I started researching domestic violence, and I found out that what he was doing was called simple obsession stalking. It means that a woman is being stalked by someone she knows: a husband, a boyfriend, a coworker, or an acquaintance. I learned that a lot of stalking occurs when victims try to leave their batterers. The more I learned, the more terrified I became—but the knowledge also made me aware of how necessary it was for me to leave!"

When Barb transcended her fear of her husband and found the courage to leave him, her life was almost immediately transformed for the better. She told us, "I feel liberated and completely free from the constant threat of my husband's dominance. Leaving changed everything for me." Barb made a move to Los Angeles, a place where she'd always wanted to live, and has returned to school to become a web site designer. She has an ever-growing network of loving friends and supportive family, but the most positive aspect of overcoming her fear has been her own life. "I am alive. Many don't get out alive."

◆　　◆　　◆

What can we do to transcend the fear of ending a dangerous relationship? Rhonda B. Saunders, Deputy District Attorney for the Los Angeles District Attorney's Office, is the woman responsible for establishing the LADA Stalking and Threat Assessment Team. In an exclusive interview, Ms. Saunders offered this valuable information on defending yourself against a stalker or a simple obsession stalker. "It's obsession, but it's not love," she stressed. "Simple obsession stalkers can be the most deadly. Tell your readers that a woman cannot keep it to herself. She needs support. She shouldn't be embarrassed; it's nothing she's done. As soon as it starts to feel the least bit threatening, they need to report it to the police. Then she has a record. A documented trail. Then we can do something. We have clout behind the stalking law now; a first time offense can be a felony."

Ms. Saunders was also adamant regarding the danger of the simple obsession stalker and getting help before it's too late. "We cannot overstate that if you are being abused, you absolutely do not deserve that treatment, and you do not have to live that way. If you can't find help locally listed in the front of your phone book—look under "Emergency Assistance" or "Community Services" for domestic violence shelters or rape crisis assistance—call the National Victim Center. Being stalked in any form is an incredibly stressful experience, and even if you feel that you can handle it, you should consider joining a support group. I find it a further testament to the courage of crime survivors that in many cases, when a victim did not find the support and understanding she needed from her community, law enforcement, and the criminal justice system, instead of giving up, she and others in similar situations founded their own support groups. Try surfing the Internet, looking for resources and information on stalking. You'll be amazed at what's available."

His Words Cut Like a Knife

"You whore! You slut! You're garbage! Do you hear me? *Garbage!*"

I remember standing in front of the mirror, staring at myself, while Dan's horrible words just kept blaring over and over in my mind. I must have heard them a hundred times before. "You're trash! I pulled you off the street! You're nothing but a stripper, a useless piece of meat!" I was crying. I hated every word, but I couldn't stop it! His words, each one was cutting like a knife, and that's when I saw, really saw, the razor lying there on the marble sink. Dan's voice came full force with my own realization of what that shiny blade could do. "Kill yourself, bitch! That's all you're good for! *Kill yourself! Do it!*"

Dan was rich, handsome, and for a while, he'd told me exactly what I wanted to hear—that he loved me and he'd take care of me forever. But then things changed. Now I was ready to take my own life in a ski area in Colorado, one of the wealthiest, most beautiful places on earth. Oh, yes, believe me. The road to paradise can come with one big price tag. It was going to require my death. I knew that now. Dan's words kept blaring in my mind. "So you think you'd be better off without me? What are you going to do? Go back to stripping? Don't you know if you leave me, you're better off dead?! *Kill yourself!*" I was going to do it. Finally, I was going to give in because, really, what else could I do? He was right; I was useless. Dan's voice began to lash at me again, *"Kill yourself!"* I reached for the razor, one of those straight-edged things, with a very nice handle. I picked it up, holding it next to my skin.

When my inner voice spoke, it was small, almost a whisper, but it said to me, "I am stronger than this. I am stronger, and I am better than this." I tried to shrug it off. What did it, what did I know? But that inner voice, it kept getting louder, "Listen to me! I am worth something. *I am worth being alive!*"

I dropped the razor; I remember it clattering to the floor. I started making my way through the dark empty house to the bedroom. Dan was out late, living the high life. He'd expect me to be waiting. Waiting to take his hateful words, and his fists, when he came home. But I couldn't let that happen, not ever again. I remember yanking open the closet doors, grabbing a few pieces of clothing, and hauling out my old canvas bag. It was as if my inner voice had taken over, telling me, "I am strong. I can do this. I am worth it. *I am worth it.*"

I walked away from luxury that night, with nothing but my dog, my bag, and the cash I had in my wallet. A girl-friend helped me drive from the mountains to the northern California coast, and after a while behind the wheel, I started feeling tingles rush up and down my spine. It was a rush of pride in being myself. It was pride in being alive.

Tara was afraid that, in her psychologically weakened condition, the only way out of her abusive relationship would be death. "He would chip away at me; that's how it felt. He got me away from my friends, and he'd chip away at my self-esteem. I couldn't do anything right. He basically made me feel that if I didn't act in a certain way, people were going to see who I really was—the trash he said I was when he found me. I grew up in an abusive home, and when Dan started abusing me, it was the last straw. I hated myself, and I wanted to die."

In transcending her fear of taking her own life, Tara found the courage to escape her abusive boyfriend and move safely to San Francisco. Once there, Tara began to pursue a rewarding career. "Although I'd spent some of my work life as a stripper, I'd also attended college and had some experience in retail," Tara told us. "I was really determined. I started reading books on job interviews, bought a new suit, and forced myself to send out ten résumés a day. I even turned some job offers down until I found the right one." In return, the validation of a good paying job gave her a new confidence when it came to dating and in making certain she didn't settle for less than she deserved. Tara has finally met a man who is encouraging, and compassionate, and understands her needs. As she said, "You can do anything *if* you think you're worth it."

◆　　◆　　◆

What can we do if faced with an abusive relationship? We have compiled several warning signs of an abusive partner found on the *OnHealth.com.* web site. If you can answer "yes" to any of these questions you may be in an abusive relationship: Is someone trying to control you?

Is someone trying to control your finances? Is someone becoming jealous and/or obsessive about you? Is someone calling you names? Is someone isolating you from your friends or family? Is someone threatening to hurt you, or your children, or your pets?[2]

There is a growing network of organizations (many of them nonprofit) to assist women. For instance, the YWCA provides shelter for women and their families, and offers a spectrum of employment and education services, such as GED classes, adult education, welfare-to-work programs, employable skills training, and career counseling.[3]

I STAYED FOR THE CHILDREN

We are standing across from each other, separated by the width of our bed. Your .357 magnum is pointed directly at my head. I hear nothing, feel nothing, smell nothing; my senses are shutting down, one by one. These last few seconds move in slow motion as I witness my life as if it's somebody else's while looking down the narrow barrel of your gun. Your revolver looks cold and soulless, like you, standing behind it. Silent and unblinking, my mind is rational and calm. Sixteen abusive years have led us to this, and your point is perfectly clear: "I'm going to shoot you, our children, and then myself." The last realization I may ever have is this: "*You* are my enemy, not your gun." During your rampage, you destroyed our home again, but what's different today is that you swallowed two bottles of pills. I've never seen you under the influence of a drug before.

Poison is spreading through your veins, and I can see the beads of sweat on your brow. Your pupils grow more erratic, and the gun begins to shake. All I can do is wait. I think to myself, "Thank God, I got the children out of the house, or we would all surely die." With this I feel a peaceful acceptance as I wait for the bullet in my brain.

And then I watch you pass out while standing up on your own two feet. Your body just collapses, and you fall over in a heap. I'm still alive, and I am going to stay alive. I walk around to your side of the bed and step over you, knowing I can finally leave.

Anna was afraid that her husband, a law enforcement officer, would kill both her and her children, if she ever tried to leave him. As she told us, "I was pregnant when the beatings started. He would tell me, 'You know you can't live without me because no one else would want you. You're fat, you're ugly, you're bad in bed, and you have four kids.' And I believed him. I thought that in order to protect my children, I had to stay with him."

When Anna transcended the fear that her husband would kill both her and their children, she also found the courage to begin a new life. Anna told us, "That day, while my husband was still passed out, I called my pastor from the house, and he wasn't in, because amazingly, he was standing at the front door! I knew then that God was protecting me every step of the way and caring for us all. I finally knew that I could leave and be protected." Anna went on to successfully raise her children and build an exciting career. She also met a wonderful, kind, and gentle man. They have since married and recently adopted a baby.

❖   ❖   ❖

There are many women, like Anna, who in trying to protect their children are severely battered and often killed by their spouse. In a report by the U.S. Department of Justice, a NOW study on violence against women stated that "Every day four women die in this country as a result of domestic violence . . . the most conservative estimates indicate two to four million women of all races and classes are battered each year."[4]

In an article on domestic violence made available by *Sage Publications,* the following factors were listed as warnings that your partner is prone to violent behavior: violence in the family of origin; violence as a response to loss of control; destruction of property and pets; threats of violence or death; uncomfortable or forcible sex; substance abuse; extreme, severe, and intermittent episodes of rage (with no apparent stimulus); manipulating you with lies and trying to make you feel as if you're "crazy."[5]

Nationwide, there are thousands of battered women's shelters which can be found in the phone book, through domestic abuse crisis lines, and on the Internet. The good Samaritan Battered / Homeless Center for Women with Children offers not only counseling, food, clothing, and job placement, but can also provide emergency shelter in every major city or town across the United States.[6] It takes courage to leave an abusive situation, but like Anna told us, "You have the power to leave, you just have to believe it."

ASSAULT WITH A CHAINSAW

I was sent out to a reservation in Montana to assist in a drug arrest. The territory and culture were completely foreign to me. The suspect we were looking for was male, considered dangerous, and known to have a house full of weapons. I tended to stick out in the area. There was a lot of apprehension. We had a cooperating witness that we had wired up, which means you put a wire on them and record the conversation they're having with someone, and I could hear that conversation. Things were getting pretty bad. We had word that he (the suspect) was in this house; it was truly like something out of a movie. It was a shack, small and dingy, and it was Friday. It was late in the afternoon, and it was hot and getting kind of ominous outside. There were no lights on inside; the curtains in the windows were blowing in and out, and one of the doors was creaking back and forth. I went in looking for a man who had been assaulting another law enforcement officer, with a chainsaw.

FBI Agent Kathy Hug generously shared these observations on fear in her life: "I think facing your fear enables you to get so much more out of life. When I was younger, there were things that I would not do because I was afraid of being embarrassed or of making a fool of myself. I never want to say again, 'I wonder what would have happened?' I know I would regret not trying. Fear isn't going to stop me again. I have stronger self-esteem, I think, because I tried everything. And when I failed, at least I tried." She also explained that if fear was something that held her back, she would never have gotten into this line of work. "You can't not make an arrest because you're afraid. Failing when you're making an arrest, or making poor decisions in a situation where there is no room for that could result in bodily harm or death."

Agent Hug was humble about the aforementioned story and didn't go into much further detail. The situation, however, was apparently dangerous and successful enough that the FBI, nationwide, recognized her courage. Agent Hug's supervisor put her name in for the Director's Award for Distinguished Service by a New Employee. We spoke with Agent Hug the same week she accepted her award in Washington, D.C.

In transcending her fears, Agent Kathy Hug says she feels good. She is allowed to accomplish that which motivates her: assisting the American public in seeing justice served. "Even when I've had a bad day, I still go home and think I have the greatest job in the world."

◆　　　◆　　　◆

If you are interested in pursuing a career as a Special Agent in the FBI, these are some of some of their entry requirements: You must be a U.S. citizen. You must be between the ages of twenty-three and thirty-seven *before* your appointment. You must meet vision and hearing standards. You need to possess a valid driver's license. You must be in excellent physical condition with no defects that would interfere in firearm use, raids, or defensive tactics. You must hold a degree obtained in a four-year resident program at an accredited college or university.[7]

ESCAPING RAPE

I'm in a big, old Chevy with two guys who are supposed to be taking me home. I'm seventeen years old and starting to get nervous. I don't recognize the route we're on. The driver just pulled off the main highway onto a dark, dirt road in the middle of nowhere! Did I tell anyone at the party we were leaving? Did they know who I left with? I need to stay calm, but my senses have risen to high alert. I can see the half moon, feel the humid air; there are rows and rows of corn out here in these big open fields. Stay cool, Chelsea, stay cool. I am casually going to turn my head now and look over at the driver. He turned up the music. From the corner of my eye I see the moon shining in the rear window, silhouetting the form of the guy in the backseat. He is leaning forward and leering at me. Oh, my God! He's holding a Swiss Army knife! My heart is pounding so loud I'm sure they can hear it! But who will hear me if I scream? I can't outrun them. Oh, my God, what are they going to do to me out here in these fields?!

Suddenly my instincts take over. I just know—somehow I know—that the only way to survive this is to act like I don't care. At least for now—act like I don't care; it will give me time to think of something else to do. Something, something. I can't let them see I'm afraid. If I scream or I fight, they'll rape me and kill me and throw me away in this cornfield. So, hey, it's cool. I'm tap, tap, tapping my fingers to the music. As a matter of fact, I'm humming. It's no problem. I refuse to allow either of you to see my fear! Casually, I stifle a yawn and stretch my legs. The car has stopped. The driver cut the engine and has opened his door. This is going to happen fast. I can hear the dirt crunching under his shoes as he steps around the car to me. I let my head fall to the side, bored. I have to act like I don't care. I am acting as if I'm lifeless.

"Lie down. On your back with your head toward the steering wheel."

I flop back, dead, like a fish. I say nothing. I am stretched out on the front seat, looking straight up. The driver leans down over me. I act dead. I feel the heat of his breath on my neck. I feel sick, but I can't show my fear. I can't react. He gets on top of me, breathing heavily. A hungry set of second eyes are watching us from the back. I turn my head away, eyes like glass, my face a total blank, but internally I am terrified! He struggles with his zipper. He touches my breasts. My arm falls off the seat; my hand hits the floor. My eyes are dead, my lips are dead, I am utterly still and lifeless. I can tell he's getting angry, but I can't let him see I'm afraid. I just know that I cannot reveal my terror. All of a sudden, he pulls me, hard, out of the car. I fall to the road in a limp heap. He spits out, *"What's the matter with you, bitch!?"* and drives away.

Raised to believe that listening to her intuition was silly and weak, Chelsea was afraid to heed her inner voice. "My dad thought intuition was for sissies. I adored my dad, and I didn't want him to think I was a sissy, so I adopted his way of thinking. Unfortunately, it almost got me killed—the last thing he would have wanted. That's the irony. He always thought he was protecting me by instilling toughness, but he was really robbing me of one of my strongest attributes."

In transcending her fear of trusting her intuition, Chelsea found the courage to survive her attack. As she told us, "I knew, deep down, that they were looking for a thrill. My fear would have been their thrill, and when they didn't get it, they tossed me out of the car." Trusting her inner voice has continued to have a positive impact on Chelsea's life. "I've learned that my intuition sends me signals to let me know if a situation is good or bad, like butterflies in my stomach. If I had listened to my intuition that night, I would have never accepted a ride home with those two guys because I felt the butterflies in my stomach, the apprehension, before I even got in the car, but I completely disregarded it. So now I always listen to what my body's trying to tell me."

◆   ◆   ◆

What can we do to survive a sexual assault? In a report by the *National Crime Center and Crime Victims Research and Treatment Center*, it is estimated that over 700,000 women are sexually assaulted each year.[8] Although there are no rules on how to survive a rape attack, Gavin De Becker, author of *The Gift of Fear*, says, "My best advice is . . . listen to yourself. Experts rarely tell us we already know the answers. Just as we want their checklist, they want our check." He adds, "Even when intuition speaks in the clearest terms, even when the message gets through, we may still seek an outside opinion before we'll listen to ourselves. [But] Nature's greatest accomplishment, the human brain, is never more efficient or invested than when its host is at risk." But how do we go about listening to our instincts? What do we do? De Becker suggests listening to our "messengers of intuition," such as gut feelings, anxiety, hunches, hesitation, suspicion, apprehension, and, of course, fear.[9]

PANIC IN A FOREIGN LAND

I kept thinking, "They've got our passports!" It felt like a nightmare. My mind was racing. "What if the train stops, and a scary person comes in our sleeping car, and he abducts us, and torments us, and we're raped and killed, and no one ever knows because they've got our passports!?" I could hardly breathe.

This was China on a hot dark night. It was a dirty, claustrophobic train, barreling down rickety tracks, with my best girlfriend and traveling companion asleep in the bunk below me, and I was terrified! It had been such a difficult trip. I'd had an allergic reaction to the malaria vaccination. I'd had the flu. I didn't speak Chinese. Nobody on the train spoke English. I had to calm down! I had to take care of myself! But I felt so afraid and alone. My thoughts sped on. "What if they kill us and dump our bodies next to the train tracks?" I tried to take a deep breath, but it was more like a shallow, fear-stricken pant. My mind started moving even faster. "What if we die!? What if no one ever knows what happened to us!? What if? What if!?" I had to calm down! I had to *relax!* But then I looked out the window and saw the moon.

At last, some comfort. I realized I was looking at the same moon that I've always looked at. The same moon that I've seen at home.

I'd been introduced to mind-body hypnotherapy about a year earlier, and from that kind of trance work you learn to trust yourself. You learn to trust going inside yourself. But sometimes it's hard for me to start, so that beautiful, familiar moon became a part of my transition. I knew if I could just trust myself and let my focus turn inside instead of on all the "what ifs?" a comfort would take over, physically and mentally. And it did. I just sat there in the comfort for a long time, and then I went to sleep.

Abby was afraid that, because of a prior panic episode, she'd never be able to manage another panic attack, especially in a foreign country. "Ten years earlier, when I was eighteen, I'd been traveling on an overnight train in Morocco. On an overnight train it's customary for them to take your passports, but I was very scared by that. I felt like I'd had my lifeline taken away. It was a terrible, sleepless, panicky night, and even though we got our passports back in the morning and everything was all right, when I got home I had nightmares about that Moroccan train trip. The nightmares were claustrophobic, and I'd wake up in a state of panic. After a while they went away, but I retained that feeling of uneasiness. And then when they took our passports in China, I was in my nightmare!"

In transcending her fear of not being able to manage her panic in a foreign situation, Abby now has the courage to calm herself no matter where she is. As Abby told us, "The trip to China taught me that I can soothe myself, no matter what. I can go inside myself to find comfort. Things that I fear, I'm able to do them, even knowing that the fear might come, with the knowledge that I can take care of myself. So when I might avoid something, something I'm fearful of, I'll do it now because I know I have the capacity to help myself."

◆　　◆　　◆

What can we do when we're faced with a situation that causes us to feel overly anxious? Because panic attacks can include a variety of symptoms and can develop so quickly, it's helpful to recognize what the symptoms are. From the website *anxietycoach.com,* we have compiled the following list to aid in understanding some signs of a panic attack. First, you may have physical sensations, such as labored and shallow breathing, light-headedness, tingling and numbness in the toes and fingers, chest pain, and sweating. Second, you may have strange thoughts, like "I'm dying," or "I'm going crazy." Third, you may experience overwhelming emotions, mostly of fear, shame, anger, or disgust. Finally, you may react or behave in an unfamiliar way, like holding your breath, or tensing your fists.[10]

To allay her panic attack, Abby used a method of self-soothing she'd discovered in hypnotherapy, but there are many other techniques available—from aromatherapy to cognitive-behavioral treatment to support groups to anti-anxiety medication to breathing into a paper bag.

THE MISSING PEACE

It happened for years and years. Just before I fell asleep, at the very moment when my muscles started to relax, I would have this horrible feeling that my body was being lifted up, but at the same time, this force would pull me down. I would feel really nauseated, my heart would be pounding, and I would be sweating. My eyes would be closed, but I could sense that something was there. It was an object in the shape of an uneven rectangle. On one side it was very, very sharp, and on the other side it was very, very rough. I knew that if I could just keep my eyes closed long enough, I could identify what the object was. But I wasn't ready. I couldn't face it. The fear was mental and the sensation was physical. I had to open my eyes.

I was thirteen years old when it happened. My mother, father, two little brothers, and I had been living in the bomb shelters of Israel for several weeks. One day when my three-year-old brother had to go to the bathroom, my father took him by the hand and led him to the bushes while I stood waiting nearby. I was paralyzed by the separation. As we were tiptoeing back to the shelter, right when my muscles started to relax, Lebanese terrorists bombed. Rockets and missiles exploded around us. Shrapnel fell out of the sky. My father and brother were just a few yards from me. This piece of missile flew and landed right where my dad had been standing. If he had stayed there a few more seconds, it would have literally cut my father in half. I went over there. I picked up the piece of shrapnel. It was still hot. I squeezed it so hard it burned a scar in my hand.

Years later, even after I'd moved to America, I was worried about where I could hide in our home. I felt so much fear for my own children that it made me angry. I wondered, "What am I thinking about? Why would anyone come in here?" Once I felt truly safe, and I realized what I was doing, my own curiosity gave me strength. I was finally able to keep my eyes closed long enough to explore what I had been so afraid of in my recurring dream. Once I made the connection that the object in my dreams was that piece of shrapnel, I could fully relax and once again sleep peacefully.

For me the war was over.

Eden had a terrible fear of not being able to cope with her own dark memories of war. "Israel is a completely different reality. The pattern I grew up with follows me. I had to be very aware of danger on a daily basis. I had to be very suspicious. I always had to check my path because I never knew what might be around the corner. It was a very difficult way to grow up."

When Eden transcended her fear and found the courage to face the dark secret of her childhood memory, both she and her family could finally relax. "Before I confronted my fear, although I was safe, I still felt so much fear for my children. I could hardly leave the house or leave the children with a relative to go out with my husband. The fear was becoming debilitating. Every mother needs to protect her kids, but there is a point where you cross the line, and I wasn't even aware of it. It was an unconscious thing, but once I realized where the fear was coming from, I could stop." Now Eden is able to enjoy her husband and her two young children without constantly feeling as if she will lose them. "My husband and I can go out for a romantic evening. We are all so much happier. Life is peaceful and good."

◆   ◆   ◆

Eden finally felt safe enough to confront the messages that her unconscious dream state was sending her, but some of us with this type of sleep disturbance need to pursue more structured treatment. For instance, *the-stress-site.com* tells us, "If you suffer from a sleep disorder and intend seeing your doctor about it, it's a good idea to keep a sleep diary of exactly when and for how long you are awake at night to document what's happening for the doctor and also perhaps enabling [her or him] to see a pattern. Secondly your doctor should encourage you to talk about any problems you have that are preying on your mind, creating stress and psychological trauma which is perhaps causing the problem. Not all sleep disorders are caused by psychological factors, of course, and keeping a sleep diary may help you identify any practical reasons why you can't sleep."[11]

TAKING THE BLAME

"Dad? I have something I need to tell you."

"Why are you crying, Dee? What is it?"

"This is so hard. It's been eating away at me for years. I, it's, I've been so afraid to tell you. I guess there's no easy way. I don't know how . . . I was afraid. After Mom died."

"Slow down, Dee. After Mom died, what? Tell me."

"Dad, I was raped and molested."

"When? Why didn't you tell me before?"

"The man doing it made me swear to God not to tell. I was afraid of him, so I did what he told me. I swore to God not to tell, and I thought I would burn in hell if I did. I was only eight."

"Who? Who did this to you, Dee?"

"The baby-sitter's father. At the baby-sitter's house. After Mom died. The baby-sitter's father came to visit and stayed for a long time. That's when it happened."

"Why were you afraid to tell me?"

"The baby-sitter and her whole family were always telling me that sex is a sin, that if you fornicate before marriage you are a whore. Sex is a sin because the Bible says it is; that's what the baby-sitter told me. But her father was molesting me at the same time and making me swear not to tell. I was afraid of getting in trouble because of swearing, of sinning, of sex. I thought I was bad and that it was my fault. It was confusing, and I felt guilty and afraid. I was afraid to ask and afraid to tell. I had no mother to talk to. I thought I had caused it. That's it. That's the worst part of it, of everything I had to live with. I thought it was all my fault!"

"No, Dee. No. It was never your fault."

Ever since Dee was sexually molested at eight years old, she has been afraid to tell anyone, especially her father, because she thought she was to blame. "I was just a child, and I was taught to respect my elders. Besides, when you're a kid, you trust the adults in your life and that what they are doing is right. So I thought that somehow it just had to be my fault. I became very ashamed of myself, too ashamed to ask for help, because then the adults would know I was a 'bad' girl."

When Dee transcended her fear of telling her father about the sexual abuse, her childhood wounds began to heal. She told us, "I was in my twenties when I finally told my dad, but after I did, I could ask for help. That was the main thing. I never wanted anyone to see my shame. I never wanted anyone to see my vulnerability. I was always trying to convince everyone that I could handle things like an adult. I put up so many defenses to protect myself from being hurt. But now I can appear vulnerable because I'm not trying to win anyone's approval. I'm not ashamed of myself any longer. I like me." Dee has two beautiful children, a satisfying career, a rich spiritual life, and an abundance of caring family and friends.

❖　　❖　　❖

What can we do if we know of a child who may be experiencing sexual abuse? In a report put together by *The Sexual Assault Crisis Center* of Knoxville, Tennessee, on child sexual abuse, it was stipulated that "Because most children cannot or do not tell about being sexually abused, it is up to concerned adults to recognize the signs of abuse. Physical evidence of abuse is rare. Therefore we must look for behavior signs."[12] Compiled from the same report are the following general behavior changes that may occur in children who have been sexually abused: physical complaints, fear or dislike of certain people or places, sleep disturbances, headaches, school problems, withdrawal from family, friends, or usual activities, excessive bathing or poor hygiene, return to younger more babyish behavior, depression, anxiety, running away, delinquent acts, low self-esteem, self-destructive behavior, hostility or aggression, drug or alcohol problems, sexual activity or pregnancy at an early age, suicide attempts. The main thing to remember is sexual abuse is never the child's fault![13]

To be automatically connected with the sexual assault crisis center nearest you, call toll free 1-800-656-4673.

A VICTIM FIGHTS BACK

It was a weeknight, Tuesday I think. I was alone. It was winter, and it happened at about 8:30. I was driving home and had just pulled up and stopped at the security box outside the four hundred-unit building I lived in. There were lots of big, tall trees surrounding the area, so I was always careful to look around before extending my arm out the window to the security box. That night I didn't see anyone around. The key card was in the compartment by the stick shift. I turned away just long enough to reach for it when a man's arm and head reached through the window. I saw a white rag in his hand coming toward my face. He locked eyes with me. I knew if I didn't do something fast, I might be killed.

I immediately rolled up the window, held onto the manual window handle, and put the car in reverse. I caught part of his arm and the top of his head in the window. He managed to get his head out, but I kept a strong hold on the window handle so his arm was trapped. I was afraid that if I let up on the pressure, he would try to get in the car. Once I had backed clear out of the driveway, I let go of the window handle, and he fell to the ground. I had dragged him about thirty feet.

My headlights were shining on him, and I could see him clearly out in front of me. He was lying in the road, and then he stood up. After being dragged all that way, he got up with no problem. He was wearing a nice suit and tie, and was barefoot. He just stood there staring at me. He never said a word. I drove away. When the police caught him, they discovered he had a history of break-ins and that he lived in our complex! Because there was not a mark on me and he did not say one word, I couldn't press charges. Another woman, however, did. He was in a psychiatric lockdown for a week, and we got him evicted from the apartment building.

Bell was afraid she wouldn't be able to fight back. Because she'd been assaulted before, her confidence in herself was low, and she'd spent many years feeling threatened and vulnerable. "I was assaulted by someone I was dating in high school. When I stopped wanting to go out with him, he refused to believe it. In the end, he beat me and raped me. After it happened, I became one of those people who would not stay at home alone. I'd chronically lock everything. I didn't date very often. I completely believed that I couldn't take care of myself. I was told by a couple of my friends that I should take a karate class, do something to make myself feel strong. But I was afraid to do it because I thought I couldn't do it."

In transcending her fear, Bell found the courage to take a powerful new direction in her life. "A friend sponsored me to take self-defense classes, and I finally agreed. The classes were called IMPACT. You have to learn to fight in those classes. The first time I won a fight with my instructor who was playing the part of an attacker, it felt great. It felt really great to win. And it taught me that in a bad situation not only would I fight to protect myself, I *could* protect myself." Since the attack in the parking lot, Bell's sense of confidence has been fully restored. She told us, "I am a five-foot, one-hundred-pound blonde with a history of being assaulted and raped. Why doesn't matter. What does matter is that I am a victim no more. He was the one in the dirt. This time I fought back."

❖   ❖   ❖

Like many women, Bell fought back by using the IMPACT Personal Safety techniques. IMPACT provides full-contact self-defense training for women using padded instructors who pose as assailants. They also teach verbal skills to avoid confrontation. IMPACT offers classes in most major American cities, and there is a growing number of self-defense outlets specifically designed to address a woman's self-defense needs. Experts like those consulted on *consumerlawpage.com* agree that women should be prepared for any type of attack, and the best, most effective method of preparation is self-defense.[14]

Slaying the Dragon

Fairy tales told us that the king and all of his men would protect us from the terrible dragon looming just outside the castle doors. But in some instances, it is the king himself who turns out to be the most frightening monster of all.

The fairy tales were wrong. Danger is real. It is an equal opportunity destroyer from which no one is exempt. Even superstar Madonna, who has the ability to deploy elaborate protection, is not impervious to those who would encroach upon her safety. Los Angeles Deputy District Attorney and head of LADA Stalking and Threat Assessment Team, Rhonda Saunders, was the lead prosecutor in the case against Madonna's stalker, Robert Hoskins. In an exclusive interview Ms. Saunders told us, "When I filed the charges [against Hoskins], Madonna was very scared, having nightmares. Hoskins was claiming he was Madonna's husband. But then ten minutes later he would leave a threatening note for her saying: 'If you don't marry me tonight I'm going to slice your throat.' He was extremely dangerous. Madonna was afraid to come back to California to testify against him. I had to battle with my office to subpoena Madonna; this case was not about her as much as it was about him. If he didn't hurt her, he was going to hurt somebody else, and I couldn't let that happen. When Madonna testified, she explained why she hadn't wanted to come in: 'Two reasons. Number one is, just being this close to this man who had threatened to slice my throat is making me ill. Number two, he is getting what he wants—to be near me.'" Saunders did successfully put Hoskins behind bars, but she's had to fight for justice every step of the way, at one point even admonishing her own colleagues with the chilling words, "How many dead bodies do you have to see before you understand that this [stalking] is something serious?"

Danger exists, but as women our instincts have been honed by nature to razor-sharp accuracy, and now we can use them. Living in a fairy tale gave us the kind of security that could never really exist, and some of us paid for that illusion with our most precious inherent birthright: our intuition. The ability to fear and the ability to distinguish a dangerous situation from a nondangerous situation are our most important weapons.

In an article for *Country Living's Healthy Living*, Jerilyn Ross, president of the Anxiety Disorders of America, says, "Fear is nature's way of protecting us. It's what motivates us to wear our seat belts or study for an exam. Without fear we wouldn't survive as a species."[15] Gavin De Becker, in *The Gift of Fear*, reports that some scientists believe "[The] early humans who were most afraid were most likely to survive."[16] Though we bear little resemblance to those long-ago ancestors, one thing remains true, our desire to *live*, and may we add, our desire to live *safely* with justice and dignity. Only by acknowledging our fears through awareness can we move from fear to courage.

We *are* slaying the dragon. Like the women portrayed in this chapter, many of us have survived great danger and learned to defend not only ourselves, but other women as well. As women of courage, we will prevail upon society to transcend the antiquated days of shadow and myth, and in blazing a wide new path into the future, the night sky will finally be cast aglow with the dragon's last fiery breath.

Courage and Creativity

Why Are Women So Afraid
to Take a Creative Risk?

When we find the courage to
express ourselves, we literally
cast a light on truth.

WHAT KIND OF FEAR does creativity evoke in women? Do we view creativity as something outside ourselves, a rare bit of magic that will forever belong to someone else? Or do we perceive it as our own unique method of self-expression?

Gail Carr Feldman, Ph.D., author of *From Crisis to Creativity*, writes that it was only after a terrible accident that acclaimed Mexican artist Frida Kahlo painted her first significant self-portrait. She gave the painting to her beau, but as Feldman explains, "The gift to her first love was an obvious memento. The gift to herself was less obvious but more profound: it was a declaration that she had survived. After this, Kahlo chose to be a painter rather than a doctor. Following more than thirty operations, she made bold representations of herself, each one nearly shouting that she lived, despite her wounds and emotional pain. She lived and lives on through her gift of art."[1]

For many of us, finding the courage to express ourselves—whether at home, at work, or in our relationships—is an intrinsic part of our emotional and physical survival. When we express ourselves, our innermost thoughts and desires are made manifest to the external world and given validity and strength. But finding the courage to express who we are can, at times, seem like an insurmountable task; when we voice our deepest thoughts, we may feel we're exposing ourselves to rejection. Yet sometimes our perception of rejection can be just that, *our* perception. In a 1998 interview with two-time Oscar winner Meryl Streep, Graham Fuller disclosed that even this world-renowned actress admitted to feeling nervous about an upcoming appearance on *The Tonight Show*. Her ability to share that anxiety prompted Fuller to relay to his readers, "How touching is that?"[2] When we find the courage to express ourselves, even our fears, it can be one of our most endearing and enduring qualities because we give life to what is perhaps most vital and transcendent in all of humanity—our tender, tenacious hearts.

In this chapter, we will meet women who have found the courage to express their most creative source—the infinite wisdom of their hearts. In doing that, their works shine with such illuminating truth that all who have seen them are duly inspired, if not blessed.

STAYING TRUE TO MY ART

I was more afraid than I had ever been in my life. Should I stay or just flee?

Of all the galleries in Manhattan, this was the only one where I wanted to show my work, and as I waited to see the gallery dealer, Ivan Karp, I was literally trembling. I wanted this. I really, really wanted this. I wanted him to take one look at the slides of my paintings and say, "Hey, where have you been hiding yourself?" I didn't want to fail. I'd spent the last ten years, more than ten years, failing.

It began in college. I'd attended in the mid-1970s, and at that time abstract and conceptual art were in vogue, and realistic art was not popular at all. I always loved realism—the reality of the world and what I saw around me. I had huge battles with my teachers because they were saying that realism was dead, and I wasn't exploring ideas that were current. I told them, "Yes, I am. I'm just doing it the way that I love, which is through realism." But they weren't impressed. In my senior year, they even took away my studio, and I felt completely ostracized. I would agonize over it, like something was wrong with me. It was affecting my self-esteem. I started thinking maybe I wasn't talented—

maybe I didn't have a gift. After a while, I just gave up, and I started painting abstracts to fit in.

I looked around, still waiting for the gallery dealer. Maybe I should just go? I was so nervous. I did *not* want to fail. Not one more time. Not after so many times!

I thought back to that determining point when I began to paint realism again. I'd been living in Little Italy, taking photographs of the neighborhood and the storefronts, which were amazing. And I wanted to paint them. Well, it took me until eight years after college, but I finally did. And I just fell in love with the process. I just felt like, God, this is what I'm meant to be doing. It felt right.

As I waited for the gallery dealer, another wave of nervousness hit me.

Should I be here? Maybe I should go? Maybe I'm not good enough yet.

The gallery dealer was suddenly there; I tried to smile. It took me another three years to paint these paintings, three years of my peers ridiculing me and telling me I was crazy for painting realism again. Some of them were cruel. They laughed at me. They laughed at my work, but I kept going. I was so happy to be finally painting what I wanted to paint, what I loved! The gallery dealer looked closely at one of the slides I had of my paintings. I knew he was tough. I knew he knew what he wanted.

He turned to me and said, "I'm coming to your studio this afternoon." He came to my studio and said, "I will give you a show."

At the second show he gave me, I sold a painting to the Metropolitan Museum of Art.

Susan was afraid that her work as an artist would never be appreciated. As Susan told us, "When I got out of college, I didn't have a lot of money. So I did the whole night thing—working at night bartending to pay the bills and painting during the day. I had a really hard time, and I was afraid I'd have to get a job in a gallery. It was a horrifying thought because it meant that I'd always be on the outside looking in."

Although the image of the suffering artist is common throughout history, Susan had to contend with the ridicule of her peers as well as a gender bias that still seems to permeate some of the most established, respected corners of the art world. As Susan told us, "In a sense, it's really ironic that the Met bought one of my paintings. You see, I used to have this poster hanging over my bed—it was done by a group of women artists in New York called Guerrilla Girls—and the poster said:

"Do women have to be naked to get into the Met. Museum? Less than 5% of the artists in the Modern Art Sections are women, but 85% of the nudes are female." And I loved that poster; I just loved it. It spoke to my rebellious spirit. But I never thought in a million years that I would ever get into the Met."

In transcending her fear of being ostracized by the New York art crowd and finding the courage to paint what she wanted to paint, Susan was embraced by the very people she feared most, that same New York art crowd. Because so few women painters are actually in the Metropolitan Museum of Art, Susan Holcomb has also made history, and she did it by following her creative insight and desires. Susan told us, "When I'm afraid of something, when it's really difficult for me, then I know I'm onto something. That's the thing I must pursue."

❖   ❖   ❖

How can we, in our own lives, attain new heights of personal growth and satisfaction with the power of creativity? In a recent *Psychology Today,* Robert Epstein, Ph.D., tells us, "Significant creativity is within everyone's reach—no exceptions."[3] He goes on to say that we can actually use fear to accelerate our flow of new ideas by putting ourselves in fearful situations, where we're likely to fail to some extent. It works like this: the challenging situation will bring about a resurgence of behaviors that used to be effective in similar fearful situations, but it also gives rise to new behaviors, and when the old and new behaviors begin to compete for a solution to the fearful situation, they spur creativity, new methods of problem solving, stimulation, and growth.[4]

THE VOICE OF FORGIVENESS

REHEARSAL ONE: "I send you love. I love you, Carl."

I could see him from across the stage, waiting in the wings. He was a giant of a man with a reputation for a gorgeous baritone voice—and for being mean. In the opera, *Aida*, I sang the lead and Carl played my father. In a climactic scene he confronts me and has to angrily throw me to the ground. During rehearsal for this particular scene, Carl grabbed my arms and pushed me by the waist to the ground so hard, hurting me so badly, that I ran off stage, black and blue almost immediately. I didn't know how I was going to be able to work further with such an angry person. That night, when I was home reading, there was a sentence that said if you are having problems with some-body, send them love, that we can only overcome an obstacle with love. We were two days away from opening night. I didn't like this man; he scared me. But I didn't know what else to do.

REHEARSAL TWO: "I send you love. I love you, Carl."

We were on stage and had stopped the rehearsal to discuss this scene. As Carl was preparing to grab my arm and throw me to the ground, I repeated the loving mantra over and over in my head. He began to look a little con-fused and to act a little differently, but I was still afraid. He said, "Well, how else can I do this then?" At which point I suggested a way that he could throw me to the floor without hurting me. I could see that he was begin-ning to change.

FINAL REHEARSAL: "I send you love. I love you, Carl."

We were in full, elaborate costume. He approached me, and I continued to silently repeat the words. He said, "I don't know what it is, but there's something about you; I really like you!" My fears were a little less after that, but they were generations old. Although Carl had hurt me physically, he'd humiliated me too. He'd bruised an inter-nal wound so deep that it reached out and touched all those who had suffered before me, for I am an African-

American woman who was singing the part of *Aida*, a black slave.

OPENING NIGHT:

The audience is quiet and the stage is dark; the actors are waiting in the wings. Looking into his blue eyes that night as he angrily crossed the stage, I thought, "Not in front of everyone. Please don't lose control. I send you love. I love you, Carl." As I was singing up at him, I felt his hands gently encircle my waist, allowing me to fling myself safely to the floor.

Delcina was afraid that her costar's anger would physically hurt her and also bring the production of *Aida* to a halt. Like Delcina, many of us abhor anger. When we are confronted with it in a coworker, the challenge to our creativity, as well as to our emotional diligence and intellectual resolve, can become apparent. As she told us, "Early on I had to come to grips with who I am—a black woman singing a form of music that some people can't see me doing. When I was singing in New York, everybody said my voice was beautiful, but I didn't always get hired. I knew that there were some people—not all—who couldn't see me in a certain role because I am black."

When Delcina transcended her fear of her costar's hate with love, the rest of her life was profoundly changed. In fact, her philosophy of life has become one of taking a negative experience and making it, or *creating* it, into something positive. Delcina told us, "I don't want to fight. There have been times that I have been confronted because of my race, and I haven't fought. I don't want to be angry. There are going to be people who have a problem with either my being black or my being a woman, and they will deal with it in their own way. We draw to ourselves what we most need to work on. I want to practice kindness and love. I have been told that my voice is healing. When I hear that, I feel that at least my singing has not been in vain or just for my sake. I am very interested in healing. That is how I want to live my life."

◆　　◆　　◆

How can we remain creative when faced with a difficult, perhaps even volatile work, home, or relationship situation? Julia Cameron writes in *The Artist's Way* of creative affirmations that are useful in almost any circumstance. A sampling of those are: "I am a channel for

God's creativity, and my work comes to good. As I create and listen, I will be led. My creativity always leads me to truth and love."[5] Spending time with nature, walking along the beach or hiking a mountain trail, can also provide inspiration.

A CREATIVE TEACHER IS A TREASURE

I had a running monologue in my head. "I can't do this. I can't think of anything creative, not in this short amount of time. I have to quit!" In two hours my presentation for my MA in education was due, and I couldn't give it. I was going to fail. I kept repeating silently, "I'm going to quit. I can't hold a job, go to school, go to seminars, write a thesis, keep my home going, and do a presentation! I've got to quit. I'll go back to school next year!"

Then I began to sob.

I've always wanted to be a teacher, a *creative* teacher. When I was twelve, my parents were going through a nasty divorce, and my mom suffered a brain aneurysm. She was in a coma for a month, and when she woke up, the doctors realized she'd never be able to speak again. It was devastating. This was a time when I really needed to communicate with my mom, and I couldn't. Besides my dad, who no longer lived with us, the only thing that saved me was school. I had a couple of teachers who were very creative, and they were the ones I learned from. They were the ones that sparked my imagination and helped me to see the light in my life, even when it seemed the darkest.

But now I was tired! I'd been so busy, and I couldn't think of anything imaginative that would hold a crowd. My thesis had been on literacy, and my presentation topic was on how to help parents get more involved with their kids, but I couldn't even think of how to involve myself in this project! I was still crying and walking around in a panic. I would never be the kind of teacher that I wanted to be.

Then it hit me.

While I was walking around my house, it was as if I was looking for something, looking for an idea for my presentation like it might be buried treasure! And what child doesn't want to look for buried treasure?

I had found the light in the darkness, just like my teachers had taught me.

Two hours later I presented a Literacy Treasure Hunt for parents to play with their children. On little cards around the classroom, I had written rhymes that a child could read out loud, and each rhyme held a clue to the next step of the treasure hunt. At the end of the hunt were little presents and pieces of candy. My professor loved it, and so do the parents of the second graders that I teach today.

Deanna was afraid that not only would she fail to achieve her master's in education, but that she'd never be the creative teacher she'd always aspired to be. Deanna told us, "I was afraid that I'd fail those teachers who saved me when I was an adolescent. After my mom's brain aneurysm, I was what you would call an at-risk kid. If I hadn't been inspired at school, I could have ended up in a very bad circumstance. I could have given up on my grades, my attendance, my future, just like I almost did that night of my MA presentation."

When Deanna transcended her fear of failing as a creative teacher, she found the courage to create a new method to help parents become involved in their children's literacy. Deanna told us, "The foundation of good teaching is based in creativity. It's up to the teacher to take a creative risk because that is what will spark the child's curiosity, and once their curiosity is sparked, learning becomes easy. Learning becomes fun. I'm very passionate about my kids and their achievements. Especially the at-risk kids, because I know how hard it is to learn when you're young and hurting. Kids need school, and they need the power to take control of their lives that only creative thinking can bring."

◆　　◆　　◆

What can we do when faced with the fear of failing our own creative aspirations? In her acclaimed book, *Freeing the Creative Spirit*, Adriana Diaz suggests, "Take a few moments to go back to your early memories of [creativity] and play. Do you remember playing at the beach or in a sandbox? Remember making mud pies and turning cartwheels? If you think back to the time when you played without a game board or scoring system, you will probably remember being silly and curious. Like the characters in C.S. Lewis's classic, *The Lion, the Witch, and the Wardrobe*, young children when left to their own devices will wander and explore their environment for play themes and activities. Even though most children are not taken as far as Narnia, the imagination is no doubt the earliest vehicle for the transportation of the human spirit."[6]

ACTING WITH ANTICIPATION

When was I most afraid as an actress? Oh, that was on a David E. Kelley show; Kelley is the creator of *Ally McBeal* and *The Practice.* This was a show called *Picket Fences,* which my husband, Michael, who was not yet my husband, was producing. We'd decided, because we were involved, that I would *not* do this show. At that point, I was doing theater anyway and not too much TV and besides, it's just such a tricky situation when you're a couple and you work together. What if things go wrong?

Well, guess what? They did. At least in my head.

I suppose it was inevitable that one day Michael would tell me that I should audition for a part on the show; he thought it really seemed right for me. I did audition and I got it. The show had been written by David Kelley specifically for Marlee Matlin, and I was to be her sidekick friend. I thought it was great. But on the first day of shooting, I felt myself clutch.

Not great.

This was a very physical, very highly propped episode, which had to do with Marlee being shot, and we were dressed up as paramedics, but we weren't really paramedics and it was difficult for me. Not that it was hard acting, but I couldn't relax.

I remember going to lunch and thinking, "This is really on the line. I know everyone on this show. We are friends with these people, and the dailies are going to be horrible, and they won't like me anymore, and they'll say, "*Why did we hire her? Why? Why?* Sure, she's Michael's girlfriend, but she's awful. Really *awful!*'" Then I started psyching myself out even more with, "Maybe I can't do this medium? Maybe I should just stick to the theatre? Maybe they're going to fire me! Oh, no! How humiliating! How *horrible!*" It went on and on in my head, all through lunch. I was panicking, anticipating the very worst!

After lunch I was feeling really scared. We were shooting a scene where we're getting ready to go into a school dressed in *Wizard of Oz* costumes and suddenly, without even knowing it, I was having fun. In fact, I was having so much fun that I got into the moment. Instead of looking outside the moment, wondering if the director was going to like me, wondering where the camera was, wondering if I was going to get fired, I got into the moment—and had a really good time. That was it! My fear went away because I had fun!

A couple of days later, we were at an awards ceremony with David Kelley, and he turned to me and said, "Oh, by the way. The dailies are great. You look really great."

Lisa Chess was afraid that she wouldn't be able to live up to the expectations of her friends and colleagues, and that they would never work with her or socialize with her again. Although we may not be in Hollywood working with such well-known people, the fear of peer pressure is something we've all had to transcend in our lives. As Lisa told us, "I psyched myself out completely. I didn't think I could work with all the props, so I was anticipating being terrible!" Whether it's on the job, in our social lives, or in our family life, our anticipation of what others might think can be excruciatingly painful.

When Lisa transcended her fear of humiliating herself, she found the courage to become involved in what she was doing and made a fantastic impression on both her peers and friends. In fact, not only was this particular episode of *Picket Fences* nominated for an Emmy, but Lisa was hired back for a full season as Marlee Matlin's sidekick, a role for which she had to learn sign language. As Lisa told us, "I had two weeks to learn how to sign, and it had to be accurate because many deaf people were watching the show. If I hadn't found the value in my experience with fear on that first episode, I might not have been able to do it. But I did, and I worked the whole year." We can tap our own unique sense of creativity to help us find the beauty within ourselves, and with that we can reach outward, expanding not only our imaginations, but our minds and our hearts. Lisa says the most important thing she learned from transcending her fear is: "If you invest all of what you have in any given moment, the fear will go away."

◆ ◆ ◆

When we perceive everyone to be judging us in our own lives, what can we do? In Julia Cameron's book, *The Artist's Way*, she writes of "core negative beliefs that get in our way of becoming an artist, or for that matter, becoming a truly vibrant human being." As she tells us, "None of these core negative beliefs need be true. They come to us from our parents, our religion, our culture, and our fearful friends. Our business is confronting them."[7]

Adriana Diaz writes in her book, *Freeing the Creative Spirit*, "Many of our personal beliefs about creativity and self-image have developed unconsciously over the span of a lifetime. Understanding [our true beliefs] is an important step in freeing the creative spirit. You may realize that you have been living in a false personal mythology that does not promote creativity."[8]

THE FIGHT TO WRITE

Now that I'm sitting in my backyard, everything should be just fine. I'll situate myself here under this nice shade tree and sit calmly on my favorite garden chair. But why do the palms of my hands feel clammy? Why is my heart beating so fast? Look around, Susan. Breathe; breathe. The sky is clear and birds are fluttering about, but my heart is racing. Everything feels as if it's beginning to close in on me. Something very strange is happening! How can the sky be getting dark so fast?

I lift my hands to cover my eyes. Now I cover my ears. I clench my fists and notice my knees are shaking violently up and down. I have lost the ability to prevent fear and negativity from streaming in. It feels like I'm being pulled down into an ominous black abyss! I begin to scream inside for it all just to stop. The last of my control is slipping away! It's going . . . it's going. I can feel the adrenalin rushing from my head to my hands, down my legs. All my fears have collided into one and landed in the pit of my stomach as I think: "Everything I ever dreamed of is going. It's going! I'm going to lose this house! I'm going to lose everything because I'm never going to work again!"

Suddenly, sickening heartache shakes me to the very core of my soul as I realize the jobs are no longer coming in and neither are the ideas. I imagine my home and my life as I know it disappearing like a puff of smoke. The shaking of my knees has stopped and I'm crying, aware that my body's clutched in a ball. My greatest fear, my deepest sorrow, the greatest love of my life is gone: I fear that I've lost the ability to write. Self-expression, my release, my inner self are dead and gone. And I wonder—maybe all I ever was, was afraid. Worse yet, maybe the ability to write was never really there at all. Maybe I was just a fraud. Accept it. Surrender. Breathe, Susan, breathe. Move on.

With this surrender, I become aware of a kind of peace. My contorted face begins to relax. My ears are no longer ringing and my skin, it feels a cool breeze. My knees are clenched up to my chest, so I slowly lower my feet. I wipe the tears from my face and slowly lift my chin. I open my eyes and see the blue sky. I take a deep breath and notice as I blow it out how it matches the sway in the trees. I feel the roots of the plants around me as though they are growing directly under my feet. The particles and light that filter in the air somehow seem a part of me. The warmth of the sun reaches inside my chest, calming the endless shores of my soul. The universal forces of nature and I are, in this moment of clarity, one and the same. I catch my breath and look up to the sky, so threatening a moment ago, and see it through different eyes. I have surrendered my control; I watch it blow away with the gentle breeze. Finally I've released the fear of not being able to write again. Complete surrender, and with it comes peace.

Susan was afraid that if she couldn't write she would lose everything. Having worked on many sitcoms, including *Cybill*, starring Cybill Shepherd, Susan was a very successful television writer. But as she told us, "I was never really allowed to express my authentic self as a child. Subsequently, I would experience terrible insecurity and this really devastating need for approval. I was like a doormat. In college, I would even write people's term papers to get them to like me."

Although we may not be earning a living from our creative expressions, many of us have felt the same kind of hopelessness and desperation that Susan experienced. Like Susan, we need an outlet to express ourselves, but because we're often discouraged from doing so, many women throughout history haven't been able to explore their full creative potential. Therefore, it might surprise us to discover that it is an Akkadian woman, born 4,300 years ago, named Enheduanna, who is the world's oldest known author, male or female.[9]

Because Susan was able to transcend her fear of never being able to write again, she has found the courage to do just that: write, and write, and write. As Susan told us, "Ever since I let the fear go, I've been working steadily. It's all about trust now. Trust in me, trust in a higher power, and I'm not scared at all."

◆   ◆   ◆

For women, it has been proven that much of our anxiety comes from not being able to communicate how we feel, and the very act of writing about our experiences or keeping a journal can help alleviate our anxieties. From the website *www.hopes.com*, we found several helpful reflections on the benefits of journaling. For instance, "Journaling can: give you a place to express your deepest emotions and dreams. Once you have them down on paper, then you are more likely to start to deal with them. (Besides, then you aren't holding it all bottled up inside you). It can put you in touch with parts of you that need to have a voice. Remind you of those things that are most important in your life."[10]

MY DANCE TO AWARENESS

I can still hear the sound of the choreographer's voice shouting from the back of the dark theater: Clap, clap, "three, four—*and again!*" I remember waiting in the wings for my turn, then walking alone across a big stage, the wood slick and polished from thousands of eager feet that had gone before me. I would dance my routine then say my name and then, invariably, I would say something funny. I was known as the funny one; it was my shtick. I could always make them laugh. But when they were making the original tapes for *A Chorus Line*? That was different.

In the beginning, all we were told was that Michael Bennett, the Broadway director and choreographer, was thinking about doing a show about dancers. But no one knew how, or even if, the tapes were going to be used. After we danced, Michael would have us sit in a circle, on chairs, in the middle of an empty stage. He had a tape running, while from the second row of the theater he would ask a question, and everyone would go around the circle and have to answer it. They wanted us to get personal, to talk about ourselves. Well, put me on a stage and let me dance, yes, but *don't* make me talk about myself! I withdrew further and further until they watched me almost disappear. I just couldn't do it. As each person answered the question and it moved closer to me, I would make myself even crazier. I couldn't hear what anyone else was saying because I was so afraid. I finally found out that Michael Bennett didn't know what to do with me because I froze up. He was probably going to let me go.

Then, on summer hiatus, a friend took me to a Buddhist chanting meeting, where he said I could learn to apply the laws of the universe to overcome my fears. I didn't buy it. But I was having such a hard time, I decided to try it—and I learned something important.

In September, I knew the taping had resumed and that I was getting one more chance. I remember returning to that dark theater and once again dancing on that stage. Dancing had always been my oasis. I loved the feeling of liberation it gave me. Everything I knew and loved surrounded me—the sounds, the smell, the magic of a big, empty stage was so familiar. But what about me? Had I changed?

We sat down in the circle. I began to listen to the other dancers talk about what they had done all summer, and I began to chant to myself, "Just let me stay here. Let me stay right here with you. If I can just do that then they will get to the next person. And the next. And then I will just tell my story." My turn came and I started talking. I told them about my summer, and I heard them laugh. It was such a joy to my ears because nobody had been laughing. I looked around and saw smiling, supportive faces. I heard the sounds of familiar laughter. I had reached inside, and I was dancing.

Trish was afraid to let people know how she really felt. How often does this happen to all of us? We think that if we hide our true feelings, the outside world will perceive us as stronger, better, emotionally healthier. But, in fact, being withdrawn can have the opposite effect. Because Trish Garland was afraid to reveal herself, she almost lost a major role in one of the most popular Broadway musicals of all time; she almost didn't get to play Judy Turner in *A Chorus Line*. As Trish told us, "I had no idea at the time why I was so afraid to reveal myself. I think of the past and the way I was raised;

there were some issues that my family hid. But it never occurred to me that there was a pressure to repress—we just didn't talk about certain things. Then when I came back from hiatus and I chanted, I realized I'd been repressing my emotions, and I finally stopped hiding."

When Trish transcended her fear of revealing herself, she secured her part in *A Chorus Line*. She also helped develop a character and a show that are cherished in the hearts of millions of fans around the world. Trish used a method of Buddhist chanting to keep her grounded and focused. She told us, "Before I let people see the real me, I'd been so consumed in myself, so consumed in my fear, that I almost lost this monstrous hit, this historical hit, just because I was afraid of how people would perceive me. But with the chanting, I could finally tell my story instead of being afraid of it. I could just be me."

◆　　◆　　◆

In an interview in *Shambhala Sun*, author Julia Cameron said, "People often say to me, 'Your book is a Buddhist book.' That is probably because creativity is a spiritual path. You get to look at your insecurity. You get to look at your inquisitiveness. As near as I can tell, this is what happens with a grounded meditation technique: you go through all of the shenanigans of the restless nature of the mind and what you are left with is, just be. Out of being, things are made. So creativity is the act of being."[11]

FEAR OF FALLING FLAT ON MY FACE

The crowd has fallen dead silent as I start walkin' onto the stage. It's New York: The Comic Strip. I have a battle goin' on in my head. This is beyond a nightmare; this is some sort of joke, right? Yeah, and I'm the joke! Nice, I've waited my entire career to be here, so why the hell do I have to follow Jerry Seinfeld?! Well, it's too late now because I'm up to bat. I'm lining up my cue ball, and I'm ready to take my shot.

While we were waiting backstage—I was standing around with Larry Miller, Paul Reiser, just a few comedic lightweights like that—we heard the roar of the crowd's laughter after Jerry finished. They went crazy for him! I mean, let's face it, has Jerry ever *not* made somebody laugh? So he finishes, the crowd is dead silent, and I'm next in the lineup.

I start that walk across the stage, approaching that friend or foe, the mike. My teeth are stickin' to my lips, I am quiverin', and I'm prayin' that the sweat under my armpits isn't showin' up on my shirt. All the while I'm thinkin', "Thanks a lot, pal, whoever did this to me." I get to the mike; I twist and lower it. I look out into this sea of heads; it's dead silent. I'm scared to death that I'm about to bomb and fall flat on my face.

I say something, sort of mutter it, and feel this buzz in the air. I'm lookin' back and forth at the crowd, doin' my shtick, and I start to hear some chuckles. I'm thinkin', *wow*, somebody out there thinks I'm funny. And then I realize I can actually utilize the energy Jerry has left in the room! He's left them feeling so good that I can use it and make it work for me! So I tap into it and use it to my benefit. And I'm thinkin', maybe following the world's funniest guy isn't so bad. I'm talkin', and they're laughin', and they keep laughin'. And check it out, by the time I finished, they'd gone wild for me too!

Sue was afraid that if she followed Jerry Seinfeld the audience wouldn't think she was funny. As Sue told us, "In stand-up, you're as good as you make it. I was so nervous to go on after somebody really, really good. There were times I folded and felt like I wasn't as good as my peers, and I'd let the audience get the best of me. It's so easy to see someone who is nervous up there. Being a performer, I can just tell. There's nothing worse than watching somebody wilt on stage." Although Sue has chosen a profession that most of us have had very little or no experience with, we can all relate to that feeling of being under an extreme amount of pressure to perform. Whatever the circumstance, whether it be giving a presentation in front of the boss or trying to entertain a group of hungry dinner guests, we all know what it means to have to be "on." We all know how difficult it can be.

When Sue transcended her fear of failing on stage by finding the courage to use the previous comic's energy to propel her into her own act, she began to truly excel at her profession. Sue Kolinsky has become an extremely accomplished stand-up comic. She has her own radio show in New York, writes for film and TV, and works at myriad clubs in the United States and around the world. Sue is also one of the few women who has been given the honor of performing for the USO and the troops all over Europe, during Desert Storm in Kuwait, and in Yugoslavia, Iceland, and Japan. As she told us, "The USO was a pressure. These guys want to be entertained so badly, but then they see you, and they look at you like, 'You're a woman and you want to be funny?' But I held my own. I did great."

* * *

How can we use what's around us to tap our creative potential and be great? Esteemed author Milhaly Csikszentmihalyi offers some valuable insights in his book, *Creativity: Flow and the Psychology of Discovery and Invention*. He tells us, "The first step toward a more creative life is the cultivation of curiosity and interest . . . *Try to be surprised by something every day.* It could be something you see, hear, or read about. Stop to look at the unusual car parked at the curb, taste the new item on the cafeteria menu, actually listen to your colleague at the office. How is this different from other similar cars, dishes, or conversations? What is its *essence?* Don't assume you already know what these things are all about, or that even if you knew them, they wouldn't matter anyway. Experience this one thing for what it is, not what you think it is. Be open to what the world is telling you. Life is nothing more than a stream of experiences, the more widely and deeply you swim in it, the richer your life will be."[12]

PAINTING IS A TRUTH OF MY EXISTENCE

As I enter my nephew's café, I get a bit of a shock watching my work being hung. Suddenly I feel so exposed. My paintings are so personal—so much a part of me—and I'm beginning to feel weak. Maybe I need something to eat. But it's more than that. I feel afraid! It's as if I'm slipping away, just like the old days. My mother died when I was very young, and no one really heard how I felt about that. No one really listened, except my art.

My art listened.

People should be arriving soon. A part of me wants them here, and a part of me doesn't. I'm grateful for their support, but who am I to think they should set aside their day to come and see my work? Will they even understand it? For me, it is my core on canvas, or in that sculpture, or over there in that weaving on the wall. That is me, the deep, deepest part of me. But what if they don't understand me? What if they don't see me? Maybe having this show was a mistake.

It looks as though my nephew and his helpers are just about done hanging my bigger pieces. My husband, my son, both of my daughters, and my daughter-in-law will be here. My grandchildren, my sisters, my cousins, my friends will be here too. Oh, my! I have such a supportive family! How did I get so lucky? Sometimes I express sheer joy in my paintings, sometimes sadness. This is life after all, and my art is a piece of my life, a truth of my existence.

I'd better go to the car and bring the smaller pieces in. I'll carry these two, what I call my "illuminated manuscripts;" my husband adores these. And rightly so for I adore my husband. Somehow my art reflects me back to me in a beautiful way. Hmmm. I'm starting to feel a little better. Maybe carrying my own paintings inside makes me feel my art, makes me feel like an artist.

"Vilma?" I hear my name being called.

The first guests are here. Turning to greet them, my stomach turns over. Look at all these people! I feel more tension beginning to build. I slip through the crowd. There is someone I don't know. She is looking at one of my favorite pieces. I step a little closer. She says to a friend how it makes her feel inside. She seems to understand exactly what I felt, exactly what I was trying to express! I mingle a bit more with the crowd; can it really be? It seems she's not the only one who understands my work. I just heard a group of people say they think that the show accurately reflects me. It's as if they can see my spirit. I hear someone making an offer on a painting. Now I know; I'm not losing myself at all!

I feel good.

It feels good to be seventy-one years old and me.

Vilma told us, "I was always afraid of losing myself. I think I pulled my creativity out of myself almost in desperation. My mother passed away when I was very young, and my father couldn't take care of us all on his own, so we went to live with my aunt. She was very domineering and never listened to me. I desperately wanted people to know how I felt, and art expressed what I couldn't say. As I got older, I didn't want to lose myself again. I was a late bloomer. I gave my first art show at forty-four years old, but giving an art show at seventy-one years old was very scary. I was very afraid."

When Vilma transcended the fear of losing her individuality and found the courage to give an art show in celebration not just of her art but also of her truly vibrant, youthful spirit, she validated both herself and many of those women around her. Her show was a great success. As she told us, "I have always found creative ways to take care of myself. My art is very, very personal. When I'm working, everything else in my life feels strong. When I don't work, I feel weaker. I can't handle things as well. So my art makes me feel really good. It's such a deep part of me; I really get to let everything out. My shows reflect me, and they make me feel my core. They make me feel like me."

◆　　◆　　◆

Is it possible to sustain creativity throughout our lives? The *Educational Resources Information Center Digest (ERIC)* reported a growing number of studies have found that a secondary peak of creativity can often occur after the late sixties. Among the one hundred and fifty adults studied in the Long Career Study, over half began their most creative period around age fifty. It was also found that regular creative activity contributed to a sense of well-being, and that continued involvement in creative endeavors can have a positive, therapeutic effect. Late-life creativity can also promote synthesis, personal insight, and wisdom.[13]

GIVING GIRLS A VOICE

The day had come for this big meeting, the day my partners and I were going to ask the head of one of the largest entertainment agencies in the world for financial backing, and I've got to say, we were playing with really high stakes. The assistant to the head of the agency came out and asked us to follow her down a hallway. As we did, I thought back several years to the countless hallways I'd walked before, hallways that led to readings, auditions, interviews; hallways that led through studio lots. When I was an actor and a screenwriter, there were always hallways to walk. The names and the faces changed, but one thing stayed the same: I was a nervous wreck. I was always so scared! Shaking, I would barely be able to remember whatever I'd come to say. As a little girl, I gained a lot of weight, and nervousness replaced confidence. I later lost the weight, but the nervousness had stayed.

My partners and I paused for a moment to collect our thoughts as we drew closer to the agency head's door. I looked away, alone in my reverie, when something on the assistant's desk caught my eye; it was a bowl of pistachio nuts. I smiled to myself as I remembered a day, several years ago, when a writing partner and I were walking down a hallway on our way to a meeting with the head of one of the studios. We were so nervous about pitching our idea to him that, to get our mind off our fear, my partner dared me to use the word "pistachio" at some point during our meeting. I finally met her challenge at the close of the meeting when, on our way out, I commented on what an unusual green color, "sort of pistachio-colored," her date book was.

I left the echoes of the hallways of my past behind me and looked up, focused once again. "Good afternoon, ladies." As we arranged ourselves around the table, I was aware of how far I'd come but also that fear is never very far away, because I felt a tingle of anxiety just as I was supposed to deliver what we'd come to say. I reminded myself that we were in this office for a reason, and the reason was to help teenage girls. I wasn't going to give my power away; the girls needed me.

We had a good meeting. My partners and I were able to successfully describe how important creative self-expression is to teen girls, especially in building their courage and confidence. We raised a lot of money for an interactive TV network.

The fear I overcame that day serves as a good reminder of how far I have come from those teenage years of torturous self-doubt.

Hillary was afraid her past experiences with nervousness would negatively impact the most important creative venture of her life. Many of us can relate to feeling as if our nervousness will either embarrass us or possibly destroy an opportunity. And that is exactly why an interactive network like VOXXY for teen girls is so vitally important. As Hillary told us, "Although I had a lot of support from my parents, when I was in my teens I was really overweight, and people called me names like 'fanny.' That was who I was back then, and the only way I got through those adolescent years, those years that can be so torturing and so full of fear and a lack of confidence, was with creative self-expression. That's what got me through that time, and now I want to encourage it in other girls. And that's what VOXXY is all about—creative self-expression."

When Hillary transcended her fear of nervousness, she found the courage to pursue her dream of an interactive network for girls. Now it is a reality. As VOXXY's promotional material states: "VOXXY derives its name from *vox* (the Latin word for "voice") combined with "XX" the symbol for the female chromosome." Thus, VOXXY intends to give girls a voice, and it is a collaboration of some of the entertainment industry's preeminent writers, producers, and entrepreneurs, including VOXXY creator and cofounder, Kristi Kaylor, a former MTV producer; VOXXY cofounder Maxine Lapidus, a sitcom writer for *Ellen, Roseanne,* and *Home Improvement;* sports legend Billie Jean King; and Jennifer Aniston, to name a few.

VOXXY cofounder Hillary Carlip has also volunteered extensively with at-risk girls. As she told us, "We all really believe in what we're doing, that's the main thing. We believe in the idea. We have faith in it. So if there's ever a moment of fear, we remember why we're doing this—it's for the girls. That always brings me back. Always."

◆　　◆　　◆

What can we do to transcend our fear of self-expression? It has been determined that many behavioral problems in girls arise from being somehow restricted in how they express themselves. C. Diane Ealy, Ph.D., in her book, *The Woman's Book of Creativity*, writes: "Many studies have shown us that a young girl's ideas are frequently discounted by her peers and teachers . . . In response, she stifles her creativity. The adult who isn't expressing her creativity is falling short of her potential . . . Repressed creativity can express itself in overwhelming stress, severe neurotic or even psychotic behavior, and addictive behaviors such as alcoholism. But perhaps the most insidious and common manifestation of repressed creativity in women is depression."[14] According to a recent article found on the website *www.allhealth.com*, "The risk of depression among teen girls is high, and this risk lasts into early adulthood." The same article goes on to say that, "A study of young women living in Los Angeles found that 47 percent had at least one episode of major depression within five years after high school graduation."[15]

As women, it is the faith we have in ourselves and in each other that can fuel us as we strive to fulfill our dreams, our aspirations, our creative insights, and our right to express it all.

The Art of Being Alive

Creativity is a celebration of life. As women and as human beings, creativity is one of our most special talents. It brings magic into our lives. Setting a table for a romantic dinner, writing the great American novel, soothing a dispute between colleagues, devising a theme for a child's birthday—these things all represent creativity. The need to express how we feel, particularly as women, is as necessary to our existence as water, earth, air, or fire. Creativity is an elemental aspect of our survival that cannot be confined to a museum, a film, or a book. It lives within each of us. When we find the courage to express ourselves, we literally cast a light on truth.

But what happens when our creativity is taken away from us, or when our means of self-expression is restricted? As Trish Garland, the originator of Judy Turner in *A Chorus Line*, told us, "I was so afraid of what people would think of the real me, that all I could do was sit in fear, self-involved, giving nothing back. I hid my emotions behind my dance until my dance would suffer too." To be unable to express ourselves—our tragedies, our joys, our aspirations—can suffocate our soul. That kind of self-betrayal can leave us closed and ultimately forlorn and embittered for years, if not the rest of our lives.

The esteemed painter Georgia O'Keeffe relayed to filmmaker Perry Miller Adato that she knew from the time she was a young girl that she wanted to be an artist, but her family always referred to her desire as "Georgia's crazy notion."[16] Throughout history women have often been told to be quiet, that we have little of value to say and no creative sense of perspective to impart—although in each home was a hearth that was not only created by a woman, but also tended and blessed by a woman.

Creativity is an intrinsic part of a woman's soul. We are sensitive, emotional beings, and our awareness of the world around us is vibrant and eternal. Every woman has the innate ability to nurture both life and creative insight. Every woman holds a part of the divine creator within her. Every single one of us.

Notes

Courage and Love

1   Sheri and Bob Stritof, "History of Marriage," www.about.com 2001, 1.

2   Tom G. Stevens, Ph.D., "Beyond Fear of Rejection and Loneliness to Self-Confidence," http://front.csulb.edu/tstevens/c-rejct.htm.

3   Dr. Edward A. Dreyfus, "Healing: Fear of Rejection," *Self-Help Psychology Internet Magazine*, www.shpm.com.

4   Randolph S. Charlton and Irvin D. Yalom, editors, *Treating Sexual Disorders*, Jossey-Bass Publishers, 1997, 140.

5   Ibid., 264.

6   Ibid., 265.

7   Fred Branfman, "A Cooler Head Prevails: Psychologist Robert Firestone Rejects the Quick Fix for a Bad Marriage," www.salon.com.

8   Ibid.

9   Michael A. Fletcher, "America's Racial and Ethnic Divides—Interracial Marriages Eroding Barriers," www.washingtonpost.com, December 28, 1998.

10 Ibid.

11 "Gay and Lesbian Anti-Violence Project (AVP)," www.lambda.org.

12 Melody Beattie, *Beyond Codependency*, Harper & Row, Publishers, San Francisco, 1989, 12–13.

13 Ibid.

14 "The Solution/The Problem," Adult Children of Alcoholics World Service Organization, Inc., www.adultchildren.org.

15 Hara Estroff Marano, "When Planets Collide, Interview with John Gray, Ph.D.," *Psychology Today*, May/June 1997, 68.

16 Marianne Williamson, A Return To Love, "Quotable Quotes," (HarperCollins), *Reader's Digest*, August 2000, 85.

Courage and Success

1. Gloria Steinem, "Scholars, Witches, and Other Freedom Fighters," Speech at Salem State College, 1993, www.gos.sbc.edu.
2. "Women in the Workplace," Women's History—Full Text-Spring/Summer 1996, www.thehistorynet.com.
3. Robyn D. Clarke, "An Office of Her Own," *Black Enterprise*, www.findarticles.com, August 1999, 1–2.
4. Ibid.
5. William S. Frank, "The Career Advisor: Fear Checklist Calms Job Hunting Nerves," www.careerlab.com, 2000.
6. "Overcome the Fear of Public Speaking," the anxietycoach, www.anxietycoach.com, 2000.
7. Shannon Cunnif, "Reflections on Leadership: Women's Styles Enrich the Whole," *Women in Natural Resources,* Vol. 21, Number 1, www.uidaho.edu, Fall 2000, 3.
8. Gerald Corey, *Theory and Practice of Counseling and Psychotherapy,* Brooks/Cole, 1996, Fifth Edition, 134–163.
9. William S. Frank, "The Career Advisor: Fear Checklist Calms Job Hunting Nerves," www.careerlab.com, 2000.
10. Mirta Vidal, "Women: New Voice of La Raza," www.clnet.ucr.edu/research/docs/chicanas/women.htm.
11. Oprah Winfrey, "Oprah Winfrey's Commencement Address to Wellesley College," Wellesley College, www.wellesley.edu, May 30, 1997.
12. "Women-Owned Businesses: More Than Nine Million and Thriving," *Merrill Lynch Today*, April 2000, www.today.askmerrill.com.
13. John Bartlett, *Familiar Quotations,* Little, Brown and Company (Inc), Fourteenth Edition, 1968, 831.

Courage and Health

1. Megan Othersen Gorman, "Stress: Handle Stress Like an Expert," *Reader's Digest*, May 1999, 98.

2   Nancy K. Dess, Ph.D., "Tend and Befriend," *Psychology Today Online Featured Columns*, August 2000.

3   Ibid.

4   Katrina Woznicki, "Handling Stress Better Can Reduce Stroke Risk," www.onhealth.com, August 6, 1998.

5   Ibid.

6   Penny Stern, M.D., "Stress Might Cause Fat Around the Middle," *Reuters Health*, September 25, 2000.

7   Ibid.

8   Richard B. Parr, Ed.D., "Exercising When You're Overweight: Getting in Shape and Shedding Pounds," *The Physician and Sportsmedicine*, Vol 24, No 10, October 1996.

9   "Depression and Anxiety Affect Control of Blood Sugar," www.Mediconsult.com, November 12, 1999.

10 "Assisted Reproductive Technologies," Serono Laboratories, Norwell, MA, 1995.

11 Philip T. Santiago, DC, DACBSP, FACC, FICC, "Exercise: The Ultimate Anti-Aging Pill," www.chiroweb.com.

12 "Hospital Volunteers Find Rewards No Salary Can Match, Healthy Happenings," *Daniel Freeman Hospitals*, Fall 1996, 7.

13 "Friendship Is Healthy," *Fitness Magazine*, April 1999, 65.

14 Kenneth L. Woodward, "Is God Listening?" *Newsweek*, March 31, 1997, 57–65.

15 Ibid.

16 Ronald Kotulak, "Rethinking Addiction," *Chicago Tribune*, March 15, 1999, 1–7.

17 Ibid.

18 Wayne Kritsber, *The Adult Child of Alcoholics Syndrome: A Step-by-Step Guide to Discovery and Recovery*, Bantam Books, 1985.

19 Geoffrey Cowley with Anne Underwood, "Is Love The Best Drug?," *Newsweek*, March 16, 1998, 54–55.

20 Ibid.

21 Ibid.

22 Megan Othersen Gorman, "Handle Stress Like an Expert," *Reader's Digest*, May 1999, 98.

23 Geoffrey Cowley with Anne Underwood, "Is Love the Best Drug?," *Newsweek*, March 16, 1998, 54–55.

24 Ibid.

25 Nancy K. Dess, Ph.D., "Tend and Befriend," *Psychology Today Online Featured Columns.*

26 Ibid.

Courage and Danger

1 Mary Dickson, "Rape, The Most Intimate of Crimes," www.pbs.org, 1996, 1.

2 Laura Gatland, "Warning Signs of Abuse," www.OnHealth.com, October 18, 1999.

3 "Who We Are, YWCA," www.ywca.org.

4 "Violence Against Women: A National Crime Victimization Survey Report," U.S. Department of Justice, Washington, D.C., January 1994.

5 *Partner Violence: A Comprehensive Review of 20 Years of Research*, Edited by Jana L. Jasinski and Linda M. Williams, Sage Publications, 1998.

6 Good Samaritan Homeless Center, www.helpforwomen.org.

7 "FBI Employment Entry Requirements," www.fbi.gov.

8 "Rape in America: A Report to the Nation," National Crime Center and Crime Victims Research and Treatment Center, Arlington, VA, 1992, 1–16.

9 Gavin De Becker, *The Gift of Fear*, Dell Publishing, 1997, 35, 38, 383–384.

10 "How a Panic Attack Works," www.anxietycoach.com.

11 "Diagnosing Insomnia," www.the-stress-site.com.

12 "Child Sexual Abuse, The Sexual Assault Crisis Center of Knoxville, TN," www.cs.utk.edu.

13 Ibid.

14 "Survivors of Sexual Assault," www.consumerlawpage.com, 8.

15 Debra Kent, "Irrational Fears," *Country Living's Healthy Living*, March/April 2000, 114.

16 Gavin De Becker, *The Gift of Fear*, Dell Publishing, 1997, 337.

Courage and Creativity

1. Gail Carr Feldman, Ph.D., "The Art of Self Expression", www.gailfeldman.com.
2. Graham Fuller, "Streep's Ahead: An Adult Conversation with Meryl Streep," 1998, *Brant Publications*, www.findarticles.com.
3. Robert Epstein, Ph.D., "Capturing Creativity," *Psychology Today*, July/August, 1996, 41–42, 78.
4. Ibid.
5. Julia Cameron, *The Artist's Way: A Spiritual Path to Higher Creativity*, Tarcher/Putnam, 1992, 31.
6. Adriana Diaz, *Freeing the Creative Spirit: Drawing on the Power of Art to Tap the Magic & Wisdom Within*, HarperCollins Publishers, 1992, 43–44.
7. Julia Cameron, *The Artist's Way*, 36–37.
8. Adriana Diaz, *Freeing the Creative Spirit*, 51.
9. Enheduanna, "Daughter of the Moon," www.about.com.
10. Journaling, www.hopes.com.
11. Samuel Bercholz, "Julia Cameron on the Path of Creativity," *Shambhala Sun Magazine*, www.shambhalasun.com.
12. Mihaly Csikszentmihalyi, *Creativity: Flow and the Psychology of Discovery and Invention*, HarperCollins Publishers, 1996, 346–347.
13. Sandra Kerka, "Creativity in Adulthood," *ERIC Digest No. 204*, 1999–00, www.ed.gov.
14. C. Diane Ealy, Ph.D., *The Woman's Book of Creativity*, Celestial Arts, 1995, 98–99.
15. "Young Women at High Risk for Depression," www.all-health.com.
16. Perry Miller Adato, "Georgia O'Keefe's 90th Birthday," 13WNET with PBS, [13WNET, 450 W. 33rd] NY, 1977.

About the Authors

Cheryl Fischer has been a project coordinator for several child abuse organizations, and has also helped counsel at-risk families with an emphasis on art therapy. Currently pursuing a Ph.D. in psychology at Ryokan College in Los Angeles, she has also written for TV, and traveled around the world as a top alpine ski racer. Cheryl and her husband, Robert, live in Marina Del Rey, California.

Heather Waite is currently working toward her Ph.D. in psychology at Ryokan College in Los Angeles and is a certified substance abuse counselor from UCLA. Her volunteer work has included finding sober living environments for the homeless and chemically dependent, and working with people with schizophrenia. Ms Waite is former Miss Orange County and international model. She has appeared on television shows, in commercials, and previously worked in the entertainment industry. Ms Waite has written magazine and newspaper articles and is the author of *Calling California Home.* She lives in Pacific Palisades, California.

About the Press

Wildcat Canyon Press publishes books that embrace such subjects as friendship, spirituality, women's issues, and home and family, all with a focus on self-help and personal growth. Great care is taken to create books that inspire reflection and improve the quality of our lives. Our books invite sharing and are frequently given as gifts.

For a catalog of publications please write:

Wildcat Canyon Press
2716 Ninth Street
Berkeley, California 94710
Phone: (510) 848-3600
Fax: (510) 848-1326
Email: info@wildcatcanyon.com
Visit our website at www.wildcatcanyon.com

More Wildcat Canyon Titles...

IN THE DRESSING ROOM WITH BRENDA: A FUN AND PRACTICAL GUIDE TO BUYING SMART AND LOOKING GREAT
Personal Shopping advice from Brenda Kinsel.
Brenda Kinsel
$16.95 ISBN 1-885171-51-X

40 OVER 40: 40 THINGS EVERY WOMAN OVER 40 NEEDS TO KNOW ABOUT GETTING DRESSED
An image consultant shows women over forty how to love what they wear and wear what they love.
Brenda Kinsel
$16.95 ISBN 1-885171-42-0

girlfriends GET TOGETHER: FOOD, FROLIC AND FUN TIMES!
The ultimate party planner from the best-selling authors of the girlfriends series
Carmen Renee Berry, Tamara Traeder, and Janet Hazen
$19.95 ISBN 1-885171-53-6

LIFE IS NOT WORK; WORK IS NOT LIFE: SIMPLE REMINDERS FOR FINDING BALANCE IN A 24-7 WORLD
A little book of wisdom for everyone who wants to find a balance between work and the rest of life.
Robert K. Johnston and J. Walker Smith
$13.95 ISBN 1-885171-54-4

THE MOTHER'S COMPANION: A COMFORTING GUIDE TO THE EARLY YEARS OF MOTHERHOOD
Here's a book as delightful to hold (almost) as a newborn baby, and friend as true as any for every new mother.
Tracy Marsh with Sharon Hauptberger and Lisa Braver Moss
$20.00 ISBN 1-885171-59-5

SOARING SOLO: ON THE JOYS (YES, JOYS!) OF BEING A SINGLE MOTHER
Companionship, comfort, and reassurance for women with the
most difficult—but rewarding—job of all: being a single mother
Wendy Keller
$13.95 ISBN 1-885171-60-9

LIFE AFTER BABY: FROM PROFESSIONAL WOMAN TO BEGINNER PARENT
An emotional compass for career women navigating the unfamil-
iar seas of parenthood.
Wynn McClenahan Burkett
$14.95 ISBN 1-885171-44-7

STEPMOTHERS & STEPDAUGHTERS: RELATIONSHIPS OF CHANCE,
FRIENDSHIPS FOR A LIFETIME
True stories and commentary that look at the relationship
between stepmother and stepdaughter as strong, loving, and a life-
long union.
Karen L. Annarino
$14.95 ISBN 1-885171-46-3

BOUNTIFUL WOMEN: LARGE WOMEN'S SECRETS FOR LIVING THE LIFE
THEY DESIRE
The definitive book for women who believe that "bountiful" is a
way of being in this world, not a particular size.
Bonnie Bernell
$14.95 ISBN 1-885171-47-1

AND WHAT DO YOU DO? WHEN WOMEN CHOOSE TO STAY HOME
At last, a book for the 7.72 million women who don't work out-
side the home—by choice!
Loretta Kaufman and Mary Quigley
$14.95 ISBN 1-885171-40-4

Books are available at fine retailers nationwide.

Prices subject to change without notice.